ROBIN JAROSSI is a journalist and the author of *The Hunt for the 60s' Ripper* and *Murder by the Sea*. He is also an on-air contributor to true-crime documentaries on the BBC and CBS Reality. He can be found at jarossi.com

THE REAL TED HASTINGS

THE TRUE STORY OF THE COPPER AT THE HEART OF LINE OF DUTY

ROBIN JAROSSI

First published in 2023 by Mardle Books
15 Church Road
London, SW13 9HE
www.mardlebooks.com

Text © 2023 Robin Jarossi

Paperback ISBN 9781914451188
eBook ISBN 9781914451706

Printed in the UK

10 9 8 7 6 5 4 3 2 1

MIX
Paper | Supporting
responsible forestry
FSC
www.fsc.org
FSC® C171272

For the "H" in my life – all my love

Contents

Introduction   ix

1 - Line of Duty – Guilty of Being Addictive Viewing   1
2 - The Inspiration for Ted Hastings   22
3 - Watching The Bent Detectives   40
4 - 'People Choked on Their Cornflakes' –
    Further Revelations   72
5 - Fighting Corruption – The Making of Robert Mark   89
6 - AC-12 – Fictional Descendant of A10   101
7 - Colluding With Criminals   119
8 - The High Price of Confronting Bent Colleagues   133
9 - Line of Duty's Biggest Mystery   147
10 - Making a Mark – 478 Officers Removed   164
11 - Beating Corruption – The Illusion of Success   180
12 - Casefile   202

Abbreviations   231
Sources   233
Acknowledgements   235

Introduction

A cassette beeps, the sound of water being poured into a glass.

No eye contact. Everyone stares at the notes and case files before them.

The beeping finally stops. Kate Fleming or Steve Arnott says, "AC-12 interview with…"

We are, of course, in the glass box, a setting inextricably linked in the minds of millions with the TV drama *Line of Duty*.

Even more so than Ted Hastings' office or the clandestine liaisons in a graffiti-daubed underpass, it is the long interrogation scenes that the drama has perfected and made its own. They stretch the acting skills of the top stars cast in each series, pin viewers to their seats and slowly unpeel *Line of Duty*'s most stunning revelations.

The glass-box scenes are one example of the series eschewing what everyone else is doing in British TV and mapping out its own unique world, one that has thrilled critics and audiences.

In recent years several UK crime dramas have stood out – *Unforgotten, Happy Valley, Strike, The Fall, Broadchurch, Shetland, Sherlock*. *Line of Duty*'s beat is distinct from these. It is not about outsider cops, serial killers, forensics or cold cases. It has zoned in on a subject once thought alien to British policing – high-level corruption.

Line of Duty is also distinctive in drawing on real cases and controversies. While the drama and characters are more pumped up than real life – with extravagant plot twists, car chases, shoot-outs – the corruption is based on true events.

This book looks into how the drama's DNA is rooted in the real world. Its starting point is Ted Hastings, the often exasperated superintendent in charge of Anti-Corruption Unit 12. A rather straightforward boss character in Series 1, actor Adrian Dunbar soon shaped Hastings into the show's defining personality.

A native of Northern Ireland, like his character, Dunbar has breathed life into Hastings, giving the series its most quotable lines. So well did Dunbar capture the character that he added piquancy to Hastings with a little improvisation. It was he who added an unscripted additional Nativity character to one of Ted's most unforgettable outbursts. "Jesus, Mary, Joseph and the wee donkey" was soon celebrated on social and traditional media and made its way onto mugs and T-shirts.

Hastings is, of course, more than *Line of Duty*'s most expressive and richly observed character. He is its moral core. Not perfect, he makes mistakes and is vulnerable. But he never loses sight of AC-12's mission. "If I see a bent copper, I only know one way and that's full throttle."

He does not turn a blind eye, sweep things under the carpet, let sleeping dogs lie, and all those other platitudes of the complacent careerist. Until the final episode, Hastings is still grappling with his superiors and political masters, those custodians of the corrupt status quo. At the end of Series 6, Hastings is not thanked for his team's successes in uncovering malpractice and criminality in the police. He has committed the sin of exposing the force's reputation and is pushed into retirement, while AC-12 is dismantled.

Despite this bitter outcome, throughout *Line of Duty*'s 10 years Hastings remained cussed, determined and brave. It is these qualities that have caused him to be compared often to British policing's most renowned anti-corruption officer, Sir Robert Mark.

Mark was Commissioner of the Metropolitan Police from 1972 to 1977, an unpopular outsider brought in at a time when the London force was besieged by a series of scandals. Knowing he was not welcomed by the hard-nosed detectives he now commanded, Mark could have played the game and soft-pedalled on the wrongdoing being committed by small groups of bent cops. That was the tradition that preceded him. But instead, Mark said corrupt officers could expect no mercy from him and, if necessary, he would kick the whole lot of them out of the Criminal Investigation Department.

Surely, that could be Hastings talking. Mark upset the cosy corrupt practices at Scotland Yard and made enemies. Hastings has caught much of Mark's spirit. So, it is fascinating to delve into Mark's moment as a member of the policing establishment who called out and confronted corrupt colleagues, and then to trace how *Line of Duty* has fictionalised the same internecine fight that anti-corruption officers face to this day.

Jed Mercurio, the drama's writer and creator, has justifiably been lauded for such a bold and compelling series. He has said that while the drama is invented, the corruption featured in it is real. From contemporary issues facing the police ("laddering", form-filling, racism) to actual scandals (Jean Charles de Menezes, Stephen Lawrence, Daniel Morgan), it is the real headline news that adds power to the storylines.

Like a cold case review, this book delves into *Line of Duty*'s background. It shines a light on the true crimes that spark the dramas. It looks at real corruption in high places, and speaks to real ex-detectives who have, like Hastings, Fleming and Arnott, investigated bent officers. It also hears from those who have suffered for courageously confronting colleagues who were on the take.

We begin with a celebration of this brilliant BBC success and all the talent that goes into it. The following chapters take a look at the outrageous corruption that was endemic in London and that led to Robert Mark being carefully introduced into Scotland Yard. There he created A10, the real-world counterpart of AC-12, where he brought down hundreds of suspect cops.

But corruption was not defeated and it is perhaps today more prevalent than ever. It is this world that is the setting for *Line of Duty*. The storylines delve into vital questions about how people are pulled into corruption, what is needed to fight it, just how much corruption is there in high office – and where is our Ted Hastings today?

The final part of the book is a guide to *Line of Duty*, its plots, cast and all of those crucial acronyms.

At times the language as spoken by the former officers interviewed is crude. But, mother of god, surely when dealing with ruthless crooks, that's to be expected.

Be warned – there are spoilers aplenty in the ensuing pages. However, it is hoped that for anyone who has watched *Line of Duty*, revisiting the drama's outstanding moments will add deeper insight and enjoyment of what were at times devilishly twisting and intricate storylines.

1 - *Line of Duty* – guilty of being addictive viewing

'Mother of God!'

Superintendent Edward Gerard "Ted" Hastings is the folk hero of *Line of Duty*, the most thrilling – and watched – drama series on British television in the 21st century.

He is famed for his verbal zingers, or "Tedisms" – "I think you should sit down, fella, or I'll handcuff you to that desk" – and for his death stare in the interrogation room. He grinds on with a perilous, thankless job, has integrity but is no paragon of perfection. In fact, Hastings' personal life is a catalogue of calamities. His financial investments have tanked and he clings to a disintegrating marriage. He's a bit of a fossil when it comes to gender politics. He makes mistakes and (whisper it) breaks the rules (but not to line his own pockets).

"Catching criminals is tough enough, but catching coppers – God give me strength," he says, encapsulating *Line of Duty*'s disturbing theme of criminality among officers.

Despite the threats, betrayals and personal defeats, Hastings is a man who has not given up. And that has the drama's huge fanbase rooting for the fella.

Actor Adrian Dunbar has brought to life a character who can be bloody-minded (as far as his bosses are concerned) but vulnerable over six series. A native of Fermanagh, his Ulster accent is now embedded in the fabric of the show. "Dial down the Ian Paisley," says snotty lawyer Jimmy Lakewell in Series 4, one of many adversaries who try to undermine Hastings and his team.

His top investigators, Steve Arnott, played by Martin Compston, and undercover expert Kate Fleming, actor Vicky McClure, have been spat at, insulted, beaten up and framed in the line of duty. But while the focus may have initially been on these feisty younger team members, it is unquestionably Hastings who has emerged as the drama's heartbeat.

The character is, of course, just one aspect of a creative achievement that has triumphed on a number of levels.

Writer and showrunner Jed Mercurio has, first and foremost, conjured up a breathtaking drama. Trapping bent coppers is a long game full of danger, but the twists and cliffhangers in *Line of Duty* have rarely been matched. Did Lindsay Denton manage to send her email containing damaging evidence just before "the Caddy" killed her? How on earth did Sergeant Danny Waldron get shot by his own armed unit? Will PC Maneet Bindra survive after colluding with the Organised Crime Group? Millions of viewers have found it hard not to stay tuned as each jeopardy-packed storyline unfolded.

Deception and duplicity are potent ingredients for a drama, but *Line of Duty* is the motherlode of two-timing snakes. Hastings has a heated showdown with dodgy legal adviser Gill Biggeloe in *Line of Duty*'s third series. They are eyeball to eyeball in his office. On an earlier evening she has tried and failed to interest him in a relationship with her that involves taking down something other than witness statements. Now, when he refuses to relinquish an investigation into a chief superintendent, jilted Gill accuses Hastings of being too compromised to run it.

"I only see black and white," he shouts. "No grey areas in between."

While we eventually discover how mired in wrongdoing Biggeloe is, we also come to see that Hastings is wrong about grey areas. The challenge of combating networks of bent coppers is, as in real life, often not a simple fight between good and bad cops. There are shades of good and bad. When it comes to where the line of duty lies, the corruption kaleidoscope only comes in shades of grey. Everyone is compromised to some degree at some point, even Hastings, Arnott and Fleming.

Confronted by conspiracies, murders, double-crosses and ambushes, Hastings strives to live by his code. Police chiefs and politicians turn a blind eye, cover their backsides and look after No. 1, but the blunt Ulsterman doggedly pursues the criminals masquerading as police officers – "I'm the loose cannon here. If I see a bent copper, I've got to go after him, irrespective of rank or political expediency."

The shifting grey areas make *Line of Duty* compulsive. Is an innocent suspect being framed? Why is Gill Biggeloe trying to get close to Hastings? Are certain detectives being controlled by gangsters? Is Steve Arnott really stupid enough to sleep with prime suspect Lindsay Denton? And – most controversially for devotees – is Detective Superintendent Ian Buckells smart enough to be the mastermind known as "H"?

Fictional drama usually provides resolution and justice, so we want Hastings to succeed. In the real world, media headlines are clogged with unresolved policing scandals – cops being paid by criminals to destroy evidence, detectives sabotaging an investigation into the axe murder of a private eye. Meanwhile, the fallout from one of the biggest scandals to hit the Met, the Stephen Lawrence case in 1993, continues to this day.

These and many other controversies are directly referenced throughout *Line of Duty*. The drama is fictional, but the corruption is real. *Line of Duty* explores what the real-world equivalents of Hastings, Fleming and Arnott might have to go through – ignoring the sneers and threats of bent colleagues, along with other career pressures – to build cases against detectives insidiously perverting the justice system and aiding criminals.

Every city needs a Ted Hastings figure cutting through the inquiries and inquests and official reports to unravel corruption. Most real-life custodians of police accountability seem to be more Gill Biggeloe than Ted Hastings. In Series 3 she tells Hastings she won't apologise for having one eye on a good public relations image for the police. "Anti-corruption is a double-edged sword," she says. "We need to find just enough bent coppers to avoid accusations of a cover-up, but not so many that the public begin to wonder if the police can be trusted."

Line of Duty opened with what appeared at first to be a rather low-key inquiry. Fleming and Arnott are tasked with finding out whether high-flying detective Tony Gates has been inflating his clear-up rate with a practice known as "laddering". This means convincing a suspect to "wipe the slate clean" by admitting to smaller crimes, which are "taken into consideration" and may get the offender a somewhat lighter sentence. Such "administrative detections" make it appear Gates is solving more crimes than he actually is, boosting his clear-up rate. We soon realise, however, that Gates' arrogance has seen him commit worse misdeeds, which has enabled a gangster syndicate known as the Organised Crime Group (OCG) under Tommy Hunter to blackmail him.

From there the drama ballooned into what Jed Mercurio called its "meta-arc". This was the accumulation over four series of recurring themes and storylines, mainly centring on the secret collusion between criminals and corrupt officers.

Hastings' Anti-Corruption Unit 12 (AC-12) have their victories. Tony Gates' cover-up of his girlfriend's crimes is exposed, Danny Waldron's shooting of an unarmed suspect is untangled, Detective Inspector Cottan is finally unmasked as "the Caddy". It feels as though AC-12 is closing in on the crime organisation that has infiltrated all levels of policing. And yet there are always further layers to unpeel, more bent networks to unpick.

"This is beginning to feel like a life's work," Hastings says at the end of Series 4.

Line of Duty launched on BBC Two on 26 June 2012. That the new show was on trial is denoted by the fact that BBC Two is the broadcaster's niche, less popular channel and that the summer is normally the season of low viewing figures and repeats. The audience for the opening five-parter averaged 3.8 million, but it was received well enough to get recommissioned.

As its popularity grew, the drama expanded to six parts. By its second series it had become a highlight of the Beeb's early spring drama season. It switched to the more mainstream BBC One on its fourth series in 2017. By the time of the big reveal of H's identity in the seventh episode of Series 6 in 2021, *Line of Duty* was secure as the most watched drama on UK television this century.

Audacious twists, gripping car chases and shoot-outs give the drama its high action quotient. At the same time, its cast of complex characters has made it a big draw for a phenomenal line-up of actors. Lennie James as Tony Gates and Gina McKee as corrupt businesswoman Jackie Laverty were electric in Series 1. Keeley Hawes made the dowdy, lonely Lindsay Denton both ruthless and sympathetic, a performance that showed an even higher level to her acting. Next, Daniel Mays was moving as the murderous, damaged Danny Waldron.

In Series 4 Thandiwe Newton was compelling as Roz Huntley, sucked into a spiral of killing and perverting justice –

even framing her own husband – but still convinced "I'm not a bad person".

Stephen Graham menaced as the apparently out-of-control undercover sergeant John Corbett in Series 5. Most recently, Kelly Macdonald won plaudits for her performance as compromised Detective Chief Inspector Joanne Davidson, not least for what was billed as a record-breaking 29-minute interrogation scene.

These long, dialogue-heavy confrontations are a challenge for the actors and have become a hallmark of the series. Davidson's pivotal face-off with Hastings, Arnott and Detective Chief Superintendent Patricia Carmichael – another powerhouse performance, this time by Anna Maxwell Martin – took two days to film with 50 camera set-ups. The glass-box scenes begin with the familiar long *beeep* of the audio recorder, before verbal jousting gives way to confession, compelling accusations and occasionally stunning counter-accusations. Kelly Macdonald said of the experience, "Adrian [Dunbar] told me at the beginning, it's a chance for the actors to flex their muscles a little bit… And yeah, it was really daunting."

So compelling were these confrontations that they have been analysed and ranked on the internet. By the time of 2021's seven-part sixth series, *Line of Duty* had become such a televisual juggernaut that it was being feverishly picked over on social media. Line of Duty Day would start trending on the Sunday morning of transmission in the UK, and by evening, all 10 top spots on the social-media trends would be taken by viewers discussing the latest revelations from AC-12. Industry recognition came in the form of gongs, such as the Royal Television Society Award for Best Drama Series, among other accolades.

By the finale, more than half of the UK's TV audience was enthralled by events on screen, a phenomenal achievement in the era of multi-channel television. Ted Hastings was quoted on

T-shirts, *Line of Duty* was celebrated in podcasts – *Shrine of Duty*, *Obsessed with… Line of Duty* – and the show was recommended by the likes of bestselling author Stephen King, who quoted Hastings on Twitter – "Now we're sucking diesel!" – as well as *The Guardian*'s reviewer: "This is less like watching TV, and more like being abducted by it, cuffed, then dragged along." *The Sunday Times* reported that during the Covid-19 lockdown, the late Queen had become a fan. Her Majesty would apparently discuss the intricate plots with her aide, Vice-Admiral Sir Tony Johnstone-Burt.

Line of Duty had become so much a part of the zeitgeist that in January 2022 it was brilliantly harnessed by the satirical artists Led By Donkeys, who edited footage of a floundering Boris Johnson into one of the show's interrogation scenes. "Mother of God, you must think we were born yesterday, fella," Hastings chastises the Prime Minister. "Your corruption was mistaken for incompetence." Once again, the fictional world of AC-12 was being blended with real life, this time in the shape of the Partygate scandal. More than five million people watched the four-minute video on Twitter, clearly relishing the sight of Johnson getting a proper grilling from the AC-12 team as part of Operation Bring Your Own Bottle. Asked whether actors Adrian Dunbar, Vicky McClure and Martin Compston had assisted with the video, Led By Donkeys' Ben Stewart said, "I can neither confirm nor deny that."

He added rather tellingly that making the spoof had been cathartic. "When the police aren't doing their job, who do you call for? You call for AC-12."

After the conclusion of Series 6, rather controversially with the long-awaited revelation of H's identity (the not very impressive DCI Ian Buckells, splendidly underplayed by actor Nigel Boyle), came the confirmation that *Line of Duty* was the UK's most watched drama of this century. It averaged 12.8 million viewers on its final Sunday, peaking at 13.1 million at the conclusion of the epic interrogation scene.

Line of Duty is undoubtedly a popular and critical blockbuster for creator Jed Mercurio, the actors, the BBC and the makers, World Productions.

However, the series, in addition to being addictive, escapist entertainment, works on another level. Its frisson comes from a blend of superb drama with true events and controversies. Which brings us to the real Ted Hastings.

Genesis of a television blockbuster

From the outset, Jed Mercurio wanted to do something fresh and challenging with the cop-drama format.

A former hospital doctor and RAF officer, he had moved into television scriptwriting and already taken a forensic look at another national institution, the health service, in his acclaimed series *Bodies* (BBC, 2004). In that, Max Beesley played a specialist registrar, Rob Lake, who realised his boss (played by Patrick Baladi, who would later appear in *Line of Duty* as bent lawyer Jimmy Lakewell) was an incompetent surgeon who botched surgical procedures. Lake's dilemma was that he felt bound by the custom that doctors don't blow the whistle on each other. This is the kind of dramatic conflict that Mercurio would push further in *Line of Duty*. For example, in Series 3, Sergeant Danny Waldron's armed response team feel compelled not to rat him out over his suspicious shooting of an unarmed suspect.

Mercurio got a lot of motivation from his own research into policing. He was stunned, for example, to learn that police were only investigating two out of every three reported crimes. So, "target culture" crops up in Series 1, with Tony Gates initially coming under suspicion for "laddering".

It was a real scandal that inspired *Line of Duty* in the first place. In 2019 the Metropolitan Police Commissioner Dame Cressida Dick, the country's most senior officer, said she was "outraged" by the portrayal of "casual and extreme" police corruption in the show. In one of those robust Tweets for which he has become well known, Jed Mercurio replied that his original inspiration for writing it was the Met's inadvertent shooting of an innocent man and their dishonesty in its aftermath. Mercurio was referring to the 2005 shooting by police of Jean Charles de Menezes at Stockwell tube station in London. De Menezes, a 27-year-old Brazilian electrician, had been mistaken for a suicide bomber. Afterwards, police said he had refused to obey instructions when challenged, which was later found not to be true.

This tragedy is reimagined in the opening moments of the very first episode of *Line of Duty* – and it touched a nerve with the real policing establishment. Steve Arnott, pre-AC-12, is a member of an armed anti-terrorist team raiding the home of a supposed jihadist bomb-maker. The problem is that the man, Karim Ali, has been misidentified. He is not a terrorist but is nevertheless shot dead. Senior officer Chief Inspector Philip Osborne then orders Arnott's team to concoct false statements to suggest that the man acted aggressively when asked to surrender. However, when the *Line of Duty* production team submitted the script to the police for technical advice, the force replied that the fictional events depicted were "unrepresentative" and official support was denied. Instead, to ensure a level of accuracy in the drama, the production consulted retired officers, serving officers offering covert insights, and bloggers such as Inspector Gadget and PC Copperfield.

This was important, because as Mercurio explained to *The Guardian* before the first episode was broadcast in 2012, "I appreciate the value of escapism, but there must also be a platform for television fiction to examine our institutions in a more forensic light."

So, the unifying idea was set from *Line of Duty*'s opening sequence – this was escapist entertainment that resonated to corruption scandals and police wrongdoing in the real world. That is not to say it is, as the opening titles of true-crime dramas often state, "based on real events". But, along with all the audacious plot twists and thrilling car chases, *Line of Duty*'s storylines are permeated with the most shocking police scandals of recent times. It works on two levels: as gripping entertainment and as an exploration of the rather terrifying problem of corruption within senior levels of our police.

Notorious investigations that have formed the backdrop to every series have included the murders of teenage student Stephen Lawrence and private investigator Daniel Morgan. Jimmy Savile's showbiz career built on sexual abuse has featured several times. Other parallels include the killing of Maltese investigative journalist Daphne Caruana Galizia with fictional character Gail Vella in Series 6, while the wrongful 16-year imprisonment of Stefan Kiszko for a 1975 murder he did not commit inspired the framing of Michael Farmer in the fourth series. There are many further true scandals loitering with intent in *Line of Duty*.

When it comes to a role model for Superintendent Ted Hastings, you have to go back to the 1970s to find a Met Commissioner who epitomised his strong-minded integrity. Robert Mark, later knighted, staked his reputation on confronting the culture of rampant corruption in Scotland Yard's Criminal Investigation Department (CID). He is still remembered today as the anti-corruption chief who shook up a complacent Scotland Yard and rooted out hundreds of crooked cops. It is no surprise that he is often cited as the corruption-buster who is the closest frame of reference for Hastings.

There are some differences between them. Mark was a Manchester man working in London, while Hastings is from Northern Ireland and based in an unidentified Midlands city. Their ranks are very different – Mark was the Met Commissioner in charge of strategy, while Hastings is a superintendent directing investigations. Hastings is eventually suspected of being bent himself, while Mark never was.

The similarities, however, highlight a shared lineage. Both faced hostility and pariah status from fellow officers as they dug into allegations of criminality in their forces. Mark shook up the CID when he set up A10 to chase down dishonest detectives. Hastings, of course, heads its fictional counterpart, AC-12. Hastings is accused in Season 1 of being a zealot in his fervour to investigate fellow officers. Mark was similarly accused of being more interested in arresting policemen than criminals.

Like Hastings, Sir Robert Mark's mantra in the 1970s was "catching bent coppers". In their fictional and real battles to take on deep-rooted cultures of arrogant police corruption, both men relied on small teams of trustworthy officers, both faced fierce resistance, and both had successes against the odds.

Line of Duty's lonely beat

It is worth considering for a moment how unusual *Line of Duty* is in exploring police corruption.

Mercurio had admired the US series *The Shield* (2002-2008), a blistering depiction of corrupt officers in Los Angeles starring Michael Chiklis. Meanwhile, British television might have been awash with rogue detectives throwing away the rule book and whodunits in period costume, but hard-nosed corruption by those with warrant cards rarely featured. *Line of Duty* embarked on a lonely beat with its controversial subject matter.

There were a few exceptions, including the downbeat BBC Two series *Law and Order*, written by novelist GF Newman. When shown in 1978, this blew away many of the genre's cliches to show the occasional duplicity of those enforcing the law. *Between the Lines* went out on BBC One from 1992-94. This followed Detective Superintendent Tony Clark (played by Neil Pearson) of the Complaints Investigation Bureau, although copping off in the bedroom featured so much that the series was nicknamed Between the Loins.

ITV's much-loved, long-running drama *The Bill* (1983-2010) touched on bent policing in the shape of Detective Sergeant Don Beech (actor Billy Murray), who sank from accepting backhanders to becoming fully immersed in crime.

Jimmy McGovern's ITV drama *Cracker*, which originally aired in 1993-95 and starred Robbie Coltrane as criminal psychologist Dr Edward "Fitz" Fitzgerald, also featured the prejudiced rapist Detective Sergeant Jimmy Beck (actor Lorcan Cranitch).

But *The Shield* pointed Mercurio in the direction of a British drama set in a world of bent policing. *Line of Duty* has kept its whole focus on this murky and dangerous world for six – and it has been rumoured a seventh – series.

It begins with DS Steve Arnott joining AC-12 after refusing to collude in the cover-up of the police killing of an innocent man. He is in a sense exiled in the anti-corruption force, alongside his boss Ted Hastings and DC Kate Fleming. Romance does not blossom between Arnott and Fleming because the new partners realise they will have plenty to deal with in terms of perilous and tense investigations ahead. In fact, the private lives of the main cast always play a secondary role to the main event of investigating police malpractice.

Original plans to base the series in the Professional Standards office – anti-corruption's real name in a number of constabularies – and set it in Birmingham ran into opposition from the Beeb's legal advisers. Because Birmingham is a real city it was decided to fictionalise the city and unit, hence AC-12 operating as part of Central Police in "the city".

For its first series, *Line of Duty* was very much on trial with its BBC Two summer slot. However, a second series had been discussed with the BBC, and Martin Compston and Vicky McClure were optioned for another season. The plan was for a new investigation with a major adversary along the lines of Tony Gates. Although Adrian Dunbar's Ted Hastings was less pronounced than his escapades and personal problems would be in later seasons, the audience reaction to him was so good that bringing him back was an easy decision.

The character evolved from how he was originally conceived. He was intended to be a burnt-out figure, ground down by too many years in anti-corruption, doing just enough to catch small fry, but leaving serious corruption among senior figures untouched. However, the type of actor envisaged to play such a character did not emerge during casting. Instead, Adrian Dunbar came in and put his stamp on it.

Mercurio said, "The plan was for there to be antagonism with Steve and Kate because as they dig into Tony Gates, Hastings wants to pull back because it's getting too explosive. But all that got abandoned.

"We stuck with the Adrian Dunbar way of doing it, which was a fiery character who's up for catching bad guys."

Businesswoman Jackie Laverty's shocking murder in Series 1 got a big reaction from viewers, who probably did not expect a big-name actor such as Gina McKee to get bumped off so abruptly. But this established one of *Line of Duty*'s trademarks – ruthless set-piece killings in which A-list stars made their exit. Major adversaries played by Keeley Hawes, Stephen Graham and Daniel Mays would all follow that pattern.

Mercurio has said that in the first series a lot of groundwork went into creating minor characters who may never be needed if the drama is renewed but can be developed into significant players if needed. Two such from Series 1 were Ian Buckells, who made his unimpressive entrance when he replaced Tony Gates on a murder inquiry; the other was Matthew "Dot" Cottan (the nickname deriving from the character Dot Cotton in the soap *EastEnders*). He came to exemplify one of the show's most insidious corruption themes – a criminal embedded in the police.

It is quickly shown that there is something off about these two smaller characters – what Mercurio calls "foreshadowing" – when at the end of Series 1, Buckells allows Cottan to speak alone to newly arrested OCG guv'nor, Tommy Hunter. This breach of protocol allows Cottan to advise his criminal boss to enter witness protection. Both Buckells and Cottan would, of course, emerge as major villains later on.

Shooting shifted from Birmingham to Belfast for Series 2, with Keeley Hawes as Detective Inspector Lindsay Denton giving the drama its second dynamite performance from a major guest star. The opening episode starts with an electrifying night sequence in which a police convoy is ambushed, immediately placing a steely Denton under suspicion. Keeley Hawes was compelling as the formidable, calculating woman whose motives are always difficult to discern.

She was brought back in Series 3, giving AC-12 a double headache with the addition of Daniel Mays' hair-trigger firearms officer, Sgt Danny Waldron. While Waldron is instrumental in ushering in themes of abuse in children's homes and official inactivity in exposing it, along with Freemasonry as an agency of dodgy collusion, it is Cottan and Denton who become the main focus of the conflict. Their final showdown helps to make Series 3 what for many devotees is *Line of Duty*'s most outstanding season.

The "Urgent exit required" scene at the climax of that series, in which exposed Cottan calls for OCG assistance to help him blast his way out of AC-12 headquarters, did make Mercurio and his team think twice. Would this be the moment the series jumped the shark from its realistic ethos into over-the-top action fare? Vicky McClure was keen to do the sequence in which she went gunning for Cottan, as was director John Strickland, so it went ahead. The finale certainly adds a breathtaking climax and fuel to several storylines to come – in particular, who, or what, the hell was "H"?

Series 3 was a triumph, the moment when the cast really gelled and relished working together. Series 4 already had the green light. The UK audience had almost doubled during the third season, so *Line of Duty* now moved centre stage to BBC One.

Thandiwe Newton came onboard as AC-12's next foe. She was as slippery as Denton, but distinct, and presented major new challenges to Hastings and co. Mercurio described her as the "dream ticket" for the show. Again, the series kicked off with a high-adrenalin sequence in which her character, DCI Roseanne "Roz" Huntley, was introduced during a housing estate sweep for a serial killer. This series had a particularly intricate plot in which Huntley not only had her arm amputated but exposed Assistant Chief Constable Derek Hilton (actor Paul Higgins) as a high-ranking inside operative of the OCG.

The buzz around the series went up another notch when Stephen Graham joined the cast for Series 5. His credits have included landmark British and US dramas such as *This Is England* and *Boardwalk Empire*, as well as Hollywood films with Martin Scorsese – *Gangs of New York* and *The Irishman*. He was keen to join *Line of Duty* as John Corbett, an undercover cop who goes rogue to bring down Hastings, who he believes was responsible for his mother's death.

Actor Gregory Piper, who had appeared as the nasty kid and OCG courier Ryan Pilkington in Series 1, returned as adult Ryan, another seed planted early that matured for the show. *Line of Duty* was well set at this point as the most talked-about drama on British television, with speculation about the identity of "H" sweeping through newspaper features and social media. Just when it appeared Hastings would be revealed to be bent himself, Arnott and Fleming turned the tables on OCG agent provocateur Gill Biggeloe and put their boss in the clear for another series.

Kelly Macdonald's DCI Joanne Davidson was the star focus of the sixth series. *Line of Duty* was by 2021 such a media event that it was attracting international attention and 13 million viewers on a Sunday night. Macdonald, who stole the show with her gruelling interrogation sequence (which took two days to film), jokingly "no commented" her way through a light interview on the BBC Breakfast show, mimicking her character.

Series 6 concluded with the highly controversial revelation that blundering Buckells was the Fourth Man in the group of "H", the high-ranking insiders working for the OCG. Despite AC-12's success in exposing him and halting Davidson as another OCG plant forced to assist their crimes, Hastings' team was then neutered in a move overseen by newly promoted Chief Constable Philip Osborne, Arnott's dishonest boss from Series 1. This will leave anti-corruption weaker than ever, with the squad's budget slashed by 90 per cent. The message seems clear: exposing minor corruption is all very well; exposing the full extent of it in high places is not.

Fact reworked in fiction

With fine writing and plotting, Jed Mercurio has taken a powerful subject that increasingly hits the headlines – police wrongdoing – and used high-octane drama to explore it.

In this he is in a long tradition of authors who have similarly used real cases as inspiration for their fiction. Agatha Christie reworked the notorious kidnapping and killing of the toddler of aviator Charles Lindbergh and his wife, Anne, in 1932. A $50,000 ransom was demanded. This was eventually handed over, but the little boy, Charlie, was found dead. He had probably died during the kidnapping two months earlier. Agatha Christie followed the case and was affected by this shocking outcome. In *Murder on the Orient Express* she has the victim, Mr Ratchett, revealed to be a gangster called Cassetti who had also kidnapped a child and allowed the family to believe it was alive to extort a ransom. Cassetti is murdered in retribution. Perhaps this was the author exercising fictional revenge.

More often, it is fiction writers exploring disturbing crimes to gain a glimmer of understanding into how they occur. Right back in 1843, Edgar Allan Poe's psychological mystery *The Tell-Tale Heart* echoed a contemporary murder, that of elderly, wealthy Joseph White in 1830 in Salem, Massachusetts. The case fascinated observers at the time as a study of guilt and ruthless indifference to the victim.

Truman Capote's 1966 non-fiction novel *In Cold Blood* examined the murder of the Clutter family in Kansas seven years earlier. In her 1996 novel *Alias Grace*, Margaret Atwood explored the true story of Canadian girl Grace Marks, who, with another household servant, James McDermott, was tried for the murder in 1843 of her employer and his mistress.

Mass shootings, such as the one at Columbine High School in 1999, were reflected in Lionel Shriver's novel *We Need to Talk About Kevin*.

Reimagined as fiction, such shocking true events can be deconstructed to reveal some of the motivations and causes behind them.

Jed Mercurio is doing this in *Line of Duty*. It is not intended to be a police-bashing show, despite occasional claims to the contrary and official police touchiness about it. Mercurio acknowledges that police officers are generally honest and effective. Isn't that exemplified by Ted Hastings, Kate Fleming and Steve Arnott? But how is it that decent women and men who join the force, sometimes for idealistic reasons, occasionally give in to subverting the law? What happens when such dedicated officers become cynical and feel they are doing an impossible job?

The Real Ted Hastings

Across the fiction–fact threshold, a mounting crisis of corruption confronted Ted Hastings just as it once did for Robert Mark at Scotland Yard.

The fictional version begins with a small-scale AC-12 probe into DCI Tony Gates. Before long they find that Gates is entangled in something far more serious than rigging his clear-up statistics. He's actually implicated in the criminal network – the OCG – run by Tommy Hunter. In Series 2, the OCG, in addition to hijacking the police convoy, is revealed to have its hooks in the grooming of underage girls for prostitution and blackmail.

A complex web emerges in Series 3 involving Freemasons in the police, murder, and cover-ups implicating Chief Superintendent Patrick Fairbank and other senior officers.

Series 4 throws viewers a dummy. During much of the action, the OCG is absent as we follow the desperate manoeuvrings of DCI Roz Huntley. But then in episode 5, Assistant Chief

Constable Derek Hilton sets out to deflect Hastings and AC-12 from Huntley and any investigation into what is an institutional cover-up of corruption.

"Where are all the suspects, this alleged clandestine network of corrupt police officers in league with organised crime?" Hilton demands. What began as a story about dodgy police tactics in the hunt for a serial killer is eventually revealed to be another OCG power play.

As the hunt for "H" – code for a top OCG mole in the police – gathers pace, Hastings realises with a sigh that exposing this network of corrupt officers could be a lifetime's work, a never-ending pursuit.

In the real world, a similar pile-up of scandals and exposures crowded in on Scotland Yard in the 1960s and 1970s, which led to Robert Mark being parachuted in to dig out corrupt vested interests.

It had taken a while for the heat to get turned up on the Met. In 1963 there was the embarrassment of a detective sergeant, Harold "Tanky" Challenor, who stated that he had found a brick in the pocket of a young man protesting against the state visit of King Paul and Queen Frederica of Greece. This young man, Donald Rooum, was charged with carrying an offensive weapon, but eventually found by a forensic expert to have no brick dust in his pockets. Rooum, who had also been hit several times by Challenor, was acquitted by the magistrate. When Challenor and three constables were charged with perverting the course of justice, it was found that the sergeant's mental condition was deteriorating and he was unfit to plead. He was sent to a mental hospital, later resuming work for a solicitor's firm, while the three constables he was charged with went to prison. Twenty-four other victims, who had been fitted-up in similar style to Rooum, subsequently had their sentences quashed.

This case should have raised alarms about dishonest practices in the Met, but it was easy to wave away as the solitary actions of a man under stress. Instead, Scotland Yard's detectives cracked a run of extraordinary cases during the 1960s, burnishing its reputation as never before and making heroes of several detectives.

During the immediate postwar years, what has been called The Era of the Blue Lamp, it had been the bobby on the beat who was lionised. This figure was personified by actor Jack Warner in the BBC's long-running series *Dixon of Dock Green* (1955-76), itself a spin-off from the movie *The Blue Lamp* (1950).

It was the headline-grabbing cases of the Great Train Robbery in 1963, followed by the further sensational trials of the Richardson gang and then the Kray twins that made celebrities of the detectives involved. Chief superintendents Tommy Butler and Jack Slipper were celebrated for their cat-and-mouse chases with the train robbers. Another chief super, Leonard "Nipper" Reed was able to celebrate his most famous arrest in the title of his memoir, *The Man Who Nicked the Krays*.

But all the glory for the Nippers and Slippers of the Yard began to look a little jaded following a build-up of scandals starting in 1969. Where official complacency allowed the Challenor case to slip by as just a one-off by a lone officer, the revelations that followed about corrupt networks of detectives in league with pornographers and violent armed robbers could not be so easily brushed off.

While Scotland Yard showed virtually no inclination to change its structures to tackle police cover-ups, the Home Office began to feel it was time for a new sheriff in town to sort out the villains disguised as officers of the law. Manoeuvring an outsider into place in the teeth of entrenched institutional hostility was not easy, however. It would take several years to finesse Robert

Mark into the highest post, and the outright malice his presence attracted from day one is something Hastings would know well.

As the first serious effort to clean up Scotland Yard began, this is the perfect moment to open the casebook on Robert Mark – the real-world model for Ted Hastings – and how the fight against corruption went on to infiltrate Britain's best crime drama.

2 - The inspiration for Ted Hastings

'None of my people would plant evidence.
They know I would throw the book at them...
followed by the bookshelf'

Working for AC-12 makes you more unpopular than a door-to-door Bible salesman with halitosis. In every series, as they investigate suspected corrupt officers, Kate Fleming and Steve Arnott encounter the scorn and insults of police colleagues. This is as much from conscientious, hard-working colleagues as bent officers, the attitude being, *While we're out there doing real police work, you lot are knifing us in the back*.

When Ted Hastings and Arnott walk into a pub, other off-duty officers move away from them. And when Detective Constable Nigel Morton spits in Fleming's hair in front of a whole office of police officers, no one intervenes to help or take her side. Arnott's well-wishers even leave a turd in his car.

Meanwhile, Hastings has to deal with resistance and even sabotage from bigger players in the senior ranks. Gill Biggeloe, the legal adviser assigned to AC-12, wants Arnott taken off the Lindsay Denton case. Meanwhile, Assistant Chief Constable Derek Hilton – perhaps the most spineless careerist in the *Line of Duty* universe – wants to remove AC-12 from looking into his protégé Roz Huntley and give the case to a "new more impartial authority". This results in the most plodding of plods, Ian Buckells, jeering at Hastings, "You lot treat everyone like mugs. Who's the mug now?"

These tactics are not subtle. If Hastings' team is making progress in building a case against bent coppers, his OCG adversaries invariably scheme to delay, sidetrack or undermine AC-12. Having connived over two series to scale back AC-12 investigations, Gill Biggeloe goes for broke in Series 5 by misleading Detective Sergeant John Corbett into believing Hastings was involved in the death of Corbett's mother. This is to fire up Corbett to go after Hastings. This is in addition to her occasional blatant suggestions that he should retire or resign. She is outed in the end as an OCG ally.

It's always better to frame a lone individual as a "rotten apple", Hastings says at the conclusion of that series, than to expose the real institutionalised corruption. "And as AC-12 has been a constant thorn in the side of the OCG, what better rotten apple than their commanding officer, eh, Gill?"

Line of Duty is tapping into real issues of police culture and past corruption scandals here. It harks back to the early 1970s when Robert Mark, the officer whose corruption battles parallel those of Ted Hastings, first confronted criminal networks of officers in London.

On 1 May 1972, shortly after becoming Metropolitan Police Commissioner, Mark called 50 representatives of the Criminal Investigation Department (CID) into a meeting. What was the new broom going to say to them? Scotland Yard was reeling from several lurid scandals in the run-up to Mark's promotion. Detectives had been accused of taking backhanders from pornographers and extorting money from criminals. However, CID had been policing itself for almost 100 years, a cosy arrangement that allowed for all sorts of cover-ups. The Met's detectives would not now take kindly to some big head from the provinces like Mark – who was known to be something of a self-publicist – coming in and shaking things up.

Many of those who sat down to hear the new boss that day expected some placatory comments from him. Surely, now that he had got the top job in British policing, he would make all the right noises to keep the politicians happy, the controversies would become yesterday's headlines, and CID could get back to keeping its own house in order. After all, the detective branch had always had the backing of Scotland Yard's top brass.

To understand the huge pressures on Mark the day he addressed CID in May 1972, it's worth looking at the vested interests and corrupt dealings that beset Scotland Yard at that moment. Mark would have to combat these head on if he was not going to take the easy option and settle for a quiet life.

Bobbies and detectives

Where the action in *Line of Duty* takes place in the setting of Moss Heath, in an unnamed city, London's Metropolitan Police is the biggest force in Britain. Also known as the Met or Scotland Yard, today it has around 43,000 employees (including 33,000 police officers and almost 10,000 civilian staff). It will mark its bicentenary in 2029.

At the time Robert Mark found himself walking the corridors of the old Scotland Yard building overlooking the Embankment, one solidly established Met tradition that he faced was that CID was effectively an autonomous force.

Since it had been set up in 1878, CID had been in charge of its operations against criminals as well as its own administration and, crucially, discipline. The only force allowed to investigate allegations of corruption against CID officers were their own colleagues in CID. During the 1960s, four area CID commanders oversaw 2,300 detectives, while a further 1,000 detectives in specialist squads were under the orders of their own commanders. This relatively small body of (mostly) men was a force within a force. Where detectives in a provincial force who were suspected of wrongdoing would have been investigated by officers from an outside force, this did not happen with the London CID. They looked into their own mess. They were, some might say, a law unto themselves.

As we'll see in forthcoming chapters, this allowed all kinds of cover-ups and sabotage to be undertaken to derail corruption investigations – practices that would eventually be reimagined in *Line of Duty*.

CID originally replaced the Detective Department, which itself was formed in 1842. The reason for the reorganisation was a corruption scandal later in 1877. The Trial of the Detectives, as it became known, saw three chief inspectors and one inspector in the dock at Bow Street accused of being in the pay of swindlers and crooks. One was acquitted but the other three went to prison for two years, one emerging to become a private detective afterwards. The corruption scandals of modern times have a long lineage.

Interestingly, from the earliest days of the Detective Department, contact between detectives and criminals was forbidden – a dangerous liaison that would still prove controversial when Robert Mark addressed his detectives. So, right from the start, the temptation for detectives to cross over and take backhanders from the well-heeled villains they had to deal with was powerful. With bent detectives featuring alongside criminals and conmen aplenty, the Victorian age must be ripe for a *Line of Duty* prequel, perhaps featuring Ted Hastings' great-great-grandfather.

The upshot of the Trial of the Detectives was that the CID was set up with 250 men. Because it was felt the detectives needed stringent control, the CID's Assistant Commissioner was told to bypass the Commissioner and report directly to the Home Secretary. The result was that CID became a separate force from the uniformed side, with a different hierarchy and better pay. While the boys in blue had some claim to effectiveness in preventing or deterring crime, the detectives were initially regarded as blunderers and ineffective, not helped by the primitive state of pathology and forensics. The whole fictional genre of amateur sleuths – Sherlock Holmes, Hercule Poirot, Lord Peter Wimsey – would riff on this image of incompetence at the Yard.

Further scandals reinforced the tensions between uniformed and detective branches. In 1880, officers were accused of inciting a seller of abortion drugs, Thomas Titley, to commit a crime. Though they were acquitted on a technicality, the press raised alarm at the prospect of police entrapment, and the Home Secretary, Sir William Harcourt, had to assure Parliament such tactics would be avoided.

A longstanding rivalry existed between uniformed officers and detectives – each felt it was their own branch that was doing the "real" police work. Robert Mark, like several previous commissioners, was a former soldier who was sympathetic to the military structure of the Met's uniformed branch. And like several predecessors, he did not admire the autonomous CID team, which disdained the disciplined structure of the beat cops. A maverick image became associated with the plainclothes officers – burnished in newspapers and popular culture by TV series such as *The Sweeney* – but there were dangers to go with CID's autonomy. Detectives continued to have much closer dealings with serious criminals and temptation was ever-present. Meanwhile, Mark felt that the relaxation of laws relating to betting, abortion, prostitution, homosexuality and petty wrongdoing generally meant there was less scope for beat officers to take backhanders.

"It is not that they [uniformed officers] are essentially different from the CID, so much that the basic police principles of honesty and decency are not put to the much more severe test and temptation faced continually by the detective, particularly in London, the centre of lucrative crime and vice," Mark wrote in his autobiography, *In the Office of Constable*. "Moreover, the uniformed officer does not suffer the inevitable disillusion of the detective, as he sees the law fail continually… with consequent high profits for lawyer and criminal alike."

Corruption had existed in the CID from the earliest days, only surfacing in newspaper headlines when someone, such as Sergeant George Goddard in 1920s Mayfair, got greedy. In 1928 Goddard was found to have thousands of pounds stashed away, a £2,000 house and flash car, all apparently derived from bribes from nightclub owner Kate Meyrick, among others. The case prefigured the 1970s scandal in which Obscene Publications Squad officers were paid by Soho pornographers for permission to open sex shops. Goddard was sentenced to 18 months, but the trial never revealed how a humble sergeant was able to operate a fairly elaborate corruption operation without his superiors noticing.

Such scandals were rare, but hinted at a culture of ingrained venality among some officers, protected by certain senior officers who were in on the corruption.

As things stood when Mark arrived at Scotland Yard, detectives knew the rules well and, when criminal allegations against them arose, were judge and jury in their own interests. Moreover, crooked officers knew that neither their superiors nor the courts would accept the testimony of convicted criminals against them in court.

Defence lawyers and criminals taking advantage of legal loopholes and chicanery were constant annoyances for Mark, and no doubt for many other officers before and since. The result was that some detectives could not resist going to the dark side and sharing the ill-gotten riches of those they often could not defeat. The fallout, Mark noted, was "bitter resentment between the two branches and of disharmony and distrust in the police service generally".

Mark was clear that there was a need to bring the CID under proper control for the first time in nearly a hundred years. The question was, could he do it? Did he really want to take on CID as no one had ever done before? And if he tried, would he become another victim of the hierarchy's well-honed skills in obstruction, stonewalling and reputation destruction?

Lone Ranger at Scotland Yard

As he prepared to address the CID he now commanded in 1972, Robert Mark had already experienced several soul-sapping years at the Met. After a decade as Chief Constable of Leicester, he left that role following the constabulary's absorption into the county force and had contemplated early retirement. However, in 1967 he was invited by Home Secretary Roy Jenkins to become an Assistant Commissioner at the Met. Mark asked Jenkins whether the Commissioner, Sir Joseph Simpson, was favourable to his appointment. Jenkins said Simpson had loyally agreed to abide by the Home Secretary's decision – hardly a resounding endorsement. Then, just in case Mark was in any doubt, Simpson went to the trouble to write to him and made clear that his appointment would not be welcomed at the Met.

"I felt rather like the representative of a leper colony attending the annual garden party of a colonial governor and was soon left in no doubt that I was not alone in that assessment," Mark later wrote.

The frosty reception began on his first day, when he was kept waiting for half an hour before being shown into the office of Deputy Commissioner Sir John Waldron, who showed him around. He was then left alone for his first week, and saw only his personal assistant and driver. At the end of that week, the Commissioner suggested he apply for another job in Lancashire – quite the vote of confidence from his new boss.

The Met viewed itself as pre-eminent in UK policing, and its senior men did not welcome criticism or interference from outsiders like Mark. It even liked to foster its own top brass. Men such as Sir Joseph Simpson were graduates of the police college at Hendon, and he had in place as his subordinates other Hendon men. Mark, who had lectured and developed a public profile as a proponent for changes in criminal law, was poison to them – an outsider with big ideas. He was known as "Mr Clean" and the "Lone Ranger from Leicester". As he later acknowledged candidly, no one in the Metropolitan Police viewed his arrival with pleasure or approval.

Mark's arch-enemy at the Met was another ex-Hendon man, Peter Brodie. Like Mark, Brodie was an assistant commissioner, but his role as head of C department made him more powerful. C department covered crime and Brodie was in charge of more than 3,000 detectives, whereas Mark headed D department, a jumble of responsibilities including training, welfare, communications and dogs. You could say Mark was something of a dogsbody in comparison to Brodie, who represented the UK on Interpol and whose department ran its own disciplinary procedures and separate promotion boards. Brodie was one of the most powerful men in the Met, if not *the* most powerful. It is noticeable that Brodie only gets one mention by name in the index of Mark's autobiography, despite the fact that their face-off would be a titanic battle and defining moment for Scotland Yard.

In 1968, Commissioner Simpson died and consensus in the Met was that Brodie, who had followed the C department tradition as protector of CID, was heir apparent. For once, however, the Home Office had other ideas than to give Scotland Yard its way. The new Home Secretary, James Callaghan, offered the role of Commissioner to Mark. The self-proclaimed "leper" was wily enough to say, *Thanks, but no thanks*.

He told Callaghan that if he got the job, it would be a disaster – he did not yet know enough about the Met, his appointment would be bitterly resented by insiders and as a newcomer he had no friends or allies in Scotland Yard.

Today, when many political appointees are universally pilloried as chancers and unqualified dunderheads, it takes a moment to get used to the idea that when offered the biggest job in policing and the most prestigious role of his career, Mark turned it down. But that is what he did, before going home and telling his wife he had probably cooked his goose as far as his Met career was concerned. He had suggested to the Home Secretary that Deputy Commissioner Jack Waldron should get the job. Waldron was due to retire in a couple of years and the Home Office could mull over a longer-term replacement in the meantime.

That, of course, was not the end of Mark's Met career. Callaghan promoted him to be Deputy Commissioner in Waldron's place. This was, Callaghan said, Mark's chance to show what he could do. And what he could do in his new role was tighten disciplinary measures. He stopped the practice whereby a policeman convicted of a criminal offence was suspended on full pay until his appeal. Mark ensured they were immediately dismissed. He also brought disciplinary charges against officers who had been acquitted in court or against whom there were allegations but a prosecution had not been thought likely to succeed. In most cases, these officers were suspended and eventually dismissed or received a lesser penalty.

The biggest slap in the face for CID was that Mark decided that any CID man who was thought unfit to work unsupervised should be put back into uniform. "It soon became plain that of the increasing number of officers being suspended, the majority were from the CID and that the uniform branch were only too pleased to see someone deal with a department which had long brought the force as a whole into disgrace," he would state later. This was how things were done in the provincial forces, and at last Mark began to find some allies in Scotland Yard who were pleased to see that he was prepared to puncture the CID's cosy self-rule.

In November 1969, just when tensions between the detective and uniform branches were high, *The Times* published a bombshell article whose fallout would be felt for several years. The headline was "London policemen in bribe allegations". It alleged that a detective inspector and two detective sergeants took bribes for allowing a criminal to carry out his crimes. In an editorial, the paper reported a comment by one of the men under suspicion, Detective Sergeant John Symonds, that there was a "firm within a firm", suggesting these practices were not limited to the three officers named in the article.

Symonds' use of the term "firm" is telling. It's slang for a criminal gang, suggesting that the detectives were crooks with their own crew.

For Mark, this was a gauntlet thrown down. He did not think such allegations in the press were usually in the public interest, but he understood why the editor of *The Times* had ensured his paper blurted out the whole sensational story in public. If their evidence had been quietly handed over to Scotland Yard, the paper's journalists had no faith in the CID conducting a serious inquiry into them. Mark knew from his own experience and "there was plenty of evidence on our files" that *The Times* was justified in going public. He and his closest colleagues had long been sick of the way complaints of crime by Met detectives were investigated – or not investigated. When it came to allegations that might disfigure Scotland Yard's hallowed reputation, CID had proved for decades that it was skilled in the art of cosmetic surgery.

What followed did not fill Mark or many outside of Scotland Yard with much confidence either. Mark felt the Home Office's response to the crisis was "inept". He thought a senior chief constable assisted by a special team of provincial and Metropolitan officers should have been brought in to conduct a thorough investigation. Instead, once again, the Met was handed a chance to investigate itself. An internal investigation was initially given to Detective Chief Superintendent Fred Lambert, before HM Inspector of Constabulary Frank Williamson was asked to conduct a separate investigation. This was something of a mess, not least because Williamson, though a man of integrity, did not have the power to give orders to police officers or run an inquiry as he would have liked. He was constantly undermined by corrupt officers at Scotland Yard, some of whom would later be imprisoned.

Just when it looked as though Lambert and Williamson might be forging an effective alliance, Lambert was rather suspiciously replaced in May 1970 by Detective Chief Superintendent William Moody, Head of the Obscene Publications Squad. If anyone had wanted to derail an investigation into CID corruption, putting Moody in to "assist" Williamson was the way to do it. When it came to police criminality, Moody made the three detectives accused in *The Times*' report look like saints. He was running a huge corruption racket in Soho, which he did not want exposed by Lambert and Williamson sticking their noses in and asking questions.

For his part, Williamson realised that Moody was effectively blocking and stalling his attempts to get at the truth. He also quickly became suspicious of the flash car Moody drove and his lavish entertainment.

Nevertheless, the continuing investigation into *The Times'* revelations, along with new allegations against the Drugs Squad and suspensions in the Flying Squad, meant pressure was bearing down on CID. Brodie did not allow Mark to be consulted or see any papers in relation to these cases, but everyone could feel the uneasiness in the air, as though a storm was coming. The effect of all this scrutiny, Mark said, was "to cause the CID to close ranks against everyone, uniform branch, the Press, the Home Office, in fact anyone whose conduct or comment might be thought harmful to its morale or reputation".

Mark was impotent in dealing with Brodie's C department, encompassing CID, but he had a series of running battles with them. At one point he asked the Commissioner, Waldron, to force the retirement of two senior officers who had asked him to quash the suspension of a detective for alleged corruption. Waldron refused to back Mark.

In the autumn of 1971, Mark was finally able to turn the tables on Brodie and the CID. Brodie left the country for an Interpol conference. At a meeting of senior Scotland Yard officers, Waldron bemoaned the growing level of suspensions and asked why there was such a decline in police behaviour. Mark was resolute in his response: "The answer lies in the thoroughly unsatisfactory way in which the CID investigates allegations of crime against its own members."

With Brodie absent and strong support from other uniformed officers present, Waldron was shaken by the strength of feeling in the room. Mark, as the disciplinary authority present, was given the power by Waldron to sort out the CID problem. Within 10 days, Mark and colleagues Jim Starritt (Assistant Commissioner A), Henry Hunt (Deputy Assistant Commissioner) and Ray Anning (Chief Superintendent) had drawn up plans for an independent team to investigate allegations against CID – this would become A10.

Speed in working out the details and getting Home Office approval were vital to see off any attempt by Brodie's C department to incapacitate or water down the plan.

Mark had now shown what he could do, firmly establishing his credentials as a man willing to disturb the CID's self-serving autonomy. This and growing calls in the press for a Royal Commission into policing as a whole prompted the new Conservative Home Secretary, Reginald Maudling, to accelerate Waldron's retirement and appoint Mark as Commissioner. This time he accepted, acting as Commissioner Designate until April 1972, when Waldron stepped aside.

One author, David Ascoli, caught the flavour of Mark's appointment when he wrote "a Home Secretary had had the temerity to impose a provincial peasant on the praetorian guard".

The shock of the new – Mark takes control

Brodie had been passed over. He may have felt robbed, he may have been the favoured choice among the Met's self-perpetuating hierarchy, but Scotland Yard did not appoint the Commissioner, the Home Secretary did, and there had been a growing feeling among Labour and Conservative Home Secretaries that CID business as usual would no longer do – someone had to clean up the mess.

In February 1972 the press published another stunning report pointing the finger at CID. The *Sunday People* ran a story alleging that the head of the Flying Squad, Commander Kenneth Drury, had gone on holiday to Cyprus with Soho pornographer James Humphreys and their respective wives. CID argued that to suspend Drury would undermine morale. Mark countered that not to suspend him would undermine public confidence in the police. This was the final showdown between Mark and Brodie's CID. Mark ordered that Drury be suspended. Brodie shortly after went into hospital suffering from "strain" and never returned to duty. It is highly likely that Mark would in any case have removed Brodie as CID chief, perhaps giving him his own former job in charge of training, welfare and dogs.

Mark took full command of the force on 17 April 1972 and addressed CID a couple of weeks later. In between, he had announced a shake-up of CID that suggested their autonomy would be ended and uniformed commanders would be put in charge of detectives in their divisions. However, such a reform had also been implemented in 1968 and CID had blithely carried on as if nothing had changed. Any of the 50 CID representatives assembled to hear Mark's address on 1 May might have suspected that his recently announced changes were more of the same – hot air.

They might have been expecting that Mark, like Brodie, would be giving them his blind support and solidarity. If so, they were instead about to be hit by a gale-force rebuke. John Grieve, former Deputy Assistant Commissioner, remembered the occasion. "It was announced that Robert Mark was going to speak. He said that there were going to be enormous changes, that we were routinely corrupt and if necessary he'd get rid of the whole lot of us. He didn't answer any questions and he walked out. I don't actually think he really believed we were all corrupt. But he was aiming to send a shockwave through the CID – and he achieved it."

The room was deathly silent as Mark headed for the door.

The new Commissioner later recalled, "I told them they represented what had long been the most routinely corrupt organisation in London, that nothing and no one would prevent me from putting an end to it and that, if necessary, I would put the whole of the CID back into uniform and make a fresh start... I left them in no doubt that I thought bent detectives were a cancer in society, worse even than the criminals..."

The message was clear: there was going to be a full-frontal assault on the CID's ability to whitewash bent practices among its own ranks.

Nothing like this had been heard in the corridors of Scotland Yard before. For a flavour of the verbal slap he was delivering to wake up his detectives to the changes ahead, he would later recall in a BBC TV interview: "A bent detective is not only himself a wrongdoer, not only does he do irreparable harm to a body of men who little deserve to be discredited in that way, but he harms the whole fabric of public confidence and the confidence of the courts in the police. And so far as I am concerned, he will always be a prime target and he can look to no mercy at all from me."

When the interviewer asked about his reputation for being more interested in arresting bent detectives than criminals, as many in CID claimed, Mark said with a smile, "Well, I should say they are right, and I see nothing improper about that... their effectiveness depends basically on professional skill and training, and then on integrity."

And most explosively, he would also say his aim was to have a police force that "catches more crooks than it employs". In conclusion, he said, "The century-old autonomy of the CID had ended."

Outsiders

So, Robert Mark offered no placatory comments that day to CID. He was not diplomatic. He would not pay lip-service to the need for detectives to be more accountable while allowing them to carry on whitewashing their own colleagues. Not only was he going to ensure that detectives suspected of wrongdoing were investigated rigorously, but any officers who tried to thwart him would be kicked out of the detective branch.

Opposition to his plans from within CID was immediate. Someone at the 1 May encounter had a tape recorder concealed in a briefcase and captured Mark's comments. Mark said in his autobiography that he had anticipated this and chose his words carefully. The tapes were then hawked around Fleet Street newspapers with the intention of embarrassing the new man in charge. According to Mark, however, this backfired because editors took his remarks as a sign that he was serious about dealing with CID.

Once they had a chance to regroup, representatives of CID attended a less one-sided meeting with Brodie's replacement as Assistant Commissioner (Crime). This was Colin Woods, whom Mark had appointed despite Woods having no detective experience, because he wanted a uniformed outsider to oversee CID. The detectives made clear their strong opposition to the plans to regularly switch officers between CID and uniformed branches (thereby reducing opportunities for corrupt relationships to develop between detectives and criminals). A work-to-rule was threatened by the disgruntled CID delegation. The Police Federation, which represents rank-and-file officers, complained that detectives were being punished by being put in uniform.

The most serious fallout from Mark's reforms, however, was a stream of resignations by detectives accused of wrongdoing. An early and notable example was Commander Ken Drury, head of the Flying Squad, after his holiday with the pornographer hit the *People*'s front page.

It would, of course, be inaccurate to say Ted Hastings was tightly modelled on Mark, but they are unmistakably close in spirit, which is why Mark is usually cited as an inspiration for the superintendent. As viewers discovered in Series 5, Hastings, like Mark, has pedigree as an outsider. He had been a Catholic officer in the largely Protestant Royal Ulster Constabulary. Having known the discomfort of being viewed with suspicion by both his fellow officers and the Catholic community, many of whom would have seen him as a traitor during the Troubles in Northern Ireland, he then has the grit to face further hostility as an anti-corruption officer in England.

Robert Mark displayed his own determination in the face of antagonism from entrenched interests in the Met. A provincial copper from outside the Met and the Hendon establishment, Mark worked with a small, loyal team to take on 100 years of CID autonomy.

When Hastings says he is intent on catching bent coppers irrespective of political or career expediency, he is channelling Mark's uncompromising comments about CID catching more criminals than it employs.

Mark was accused of being more interested in arresting detectives than criminals; in the drama, suspect detective Tony Gates has the same feeling when he says of Hastings, "The man's a zealot."

One further likeness ties Mark to his fictional embodiment. He was called into action against embedded criminal officers who operated on a scale that would shock the public. Rotten apples do not begin to cover how far-reaching the corrupt networks were, and the scale of real-life law-breaking would seep into *Line of Duty*.

Mark's rock-solid principles played a big part in his decision to resign as Commissioner in 1977, because he could not accept the way in which his political bosses decided to introduce an independent element into dealing with complaints against officers. This came in the form of a new Police Act, which Mark opposed because he felt it handed the final say in police discipline to political appointees.

In the *Line of Duty* universe, Ted Hastings' falling-out with the powers that be is even more spectacular. By Series 6, the Police and Crime Commissioner Rohan Sindwhani and Deputy Chief Constable Andrea Wise are leaning heavily on Hastings to stop looking for "H" and a network of bent officers.

Sindwhani is concerned about the "optics" of the public knowing that AC-12 is engaged in a far-reaching corruption probe rather than a more palatable "performance review". He tells Ted, "Officers of your rank normally appreciate politics as much as policing."

Hastings' determination to go by the book to trap criminal cops, and damn the optics and politics, clearly make him an outsider in a hierarchy of careerists intent on keeping their heads down in pursuit of the next promotion.

When he doggedly keeps his team on the hunt for "H", Wise virtually gaslights him by telling him he should stop chasing phantoms.

"Your inquiry into 'H' should close," she says. "This isn't about old battles."

He replies, "The name's Hastings, ma'am. I'm the epitome of an old battle."

Such unyielding commitment to doing the job, rather than just appearing to do it, might have got an approving nod from Robert Mark.

3 – Watching the bent detectives

'That's us now'

Line of Duty depicts hair-raising acts of police criminality. Some are the high-octane sequences of pure fiction. These would include the attempted armed breakout by bent officers of Dot Cotton from AC-12 headquarters. Then there was the Mexican stand-off on waste ground between Kate Fleming and Ryan Pilkington. Or Lindsay Denton firing off the email that incriminates Dot Cotton – while he has a gun pointed at her.

These are invariably the cliffhanger moments, often finishing the episode and fuelling social-media chats and inquests in workplaces around the country the next morning.

Much of the corruption on display is not so fanciful, however, because that is where the drama injects shocking real-world events and controversies. In *Line of Duty,* we've seen attempts by high-ranking officers to derail AC-12's investigations to ensure bent officers are not caught. Assistant Chief Constable Derek Hilton stands out as the most spectacular saboteur trying to protect the Organised Crime Group. This is one example of the drama reflecting real life, the example of Bill Moody derailing *The Times*' allegations being pre-eminent here. We have seen greedy officers such as Ian Buckells having a secret fortune in property and offshore bank accounts, in return for helping criminals prosper. Such duplicity has also happened in real life. The already cited cases of George Goddard, Ken Drury and again Bill Moody are all examples of such bribery.

One of the challenging questions that *Line of Duty* raises is that where there is corruption, it is rarely down to one rotten apple, a bad 'un, as the police establishment is usually keen to emphasise. It would be difficult for Police Constable Rotten Apple to commit any substantial corruption on his own. It often requires active support from those in more senior positions, a network of bribe-taking and bribes shared, of allowing criminals to break the law and ensuring colleagues are on-side with that.

Criminal hierarchies within law enforcement is entirely *Line of Duty*'s manor. Who can be trusted? Who is clean? Is someone out to frame me? These dilemmas recur for the characters in just about every scene. But they also shook Scotland Yard during Robert Mark's years. The press, public and politicians were confronted with a crisis in policing, realising that corruption was far more serious than had ever been admitted or realised outside the corridors of Scotland Yard. In a 2010 tribute to Robert Mark, *The Guardian* wrote that at the beginning, the task he faced as the new Commissioner was vast, and that the corruption was "endemic and cynical". How Mark eventually confronted the embedded cabals of bent detectives reveals why he is such a powerful role model for Superintendent Ted Hastings.

To appreciate how big a job Mark was up against when he took control in 1972, it is worth stepping back a couple of years to see how deep-rooted corruption had become by then. A stunning report published in *The Times* on 29 November 1969 set the dominoes tumbling on several rackets that certain detectives were running. On its front page, right next to a photo of the second moon landing by Apollo 12 astronauts, was the story – mentioned in the previous chapter – headlined "London police in bribe allegations". That this was the establishment's newspaper and not the muck-raking *News of the World* making the claims gave the story all the more shock value. The prevailing feeling up to that moment was that the best police force in the world simply didn't do that sort of thing. How the mood shifted is well summed up by the comment of a criminal lawyer who read *The Times* report that morning: "Like catching the Archbishop of Canterbury in bed with a prostitute."

It had been painstakingly put together by reporters Garry Lloyd and Julian Mounter. Gathering the details involved the secret tape-recording of detectives talking to criminals in cars. *The Times*' exposé would quote Detective Sergeant John Symonds telling a criminal that he could help him because he was part of a "firm within a firm". This quote became notorious, signalling that a network of corrupt officers was running their own criminal operations within CID.

The Times alleged that at least three detectives were taking backhanders from criminals in exchange for dropping charges against them, watering down evidence offered in court, and for allowing criminals to operate without police interference. In addition to Symonds, who was based in Camberwell, it named Detective Inspector Bernard Robson of Scotland Yard's C9 Division, which investigated the spread of crime outside London, and Detective Sergeant Gordon Harris, a regional crime squad officer on detachment from Brighton. These three had, it was stated, pocketed more than £400 between them in the previous month alone (equivalent to £4,700 today).

The reporting team had also photographed meetings between the detectives and a young criminal, who it did not name but was actually a 22-year-old car dealer with a string of convictions called Michael Roy Perry. One of the transactions recorded was for £50 (today: approximately £600) for getting Perry off a possible charge of theft.

In *Line of Duty*, the Organised Crime Group's favourite tactic for entrapping detectives into colluding with them is to plant the officer's DNA on a murder victim. The victim's body is then stored in a freezer, as happened with Jackie Laverty. If the fictional detective does not cooperate, the body is allowed to be found with their incriminating DNA on it. Michael Perry was snared in a similar way back in 1969, though it was his fingerprints that were used against him. Robson tricked Perry into taking hold of what he said was a piece of gelignite, thereby leaving his fingerprints on it. These could then be used to frame him as a safe-breaker. Perry ended up handing over £200 (£2,300 today) to Harris and Robson to ensure there would be no criminal charge for possessing the gelignite.

Another corrupt deal proposed by DS Harris and DI Robson was that Perry could plant stolen cigarettes in a sweet shop owned by an enemy of Perry's. "If there's anyone who's ever done you a mischief…" Robson said, "that wants seeing to, you know what I mean?" The detectives would then raid the shop and either extort money from the store owner or charge him. Any money obtained from the shopkeeper would be shared with Perry.

"Then we'll go in and if it's a good load he's taken, then he can bloody well pay and we'll give you fair shares," DI Robson said to Perry.

DS Symonds, operating separately from Robson and Harris, offered to give Perry "a licence". Pay a fee and the detective would turn a blind eye to his crimes. He is reported as saying, "… round here, any time – anything you like, anything. Might give you a licence."

The detective offers to divert police from the area where he might commit a crime and even offered to join him on the job if there was enough money in it. "If it's big, I'll come with you," he told Perry, "… you can't have better insurance than that." Such a ringing endorsement of the service the sergeant was offering. Symonds had clearly worked out all the angles, even suggesting they have a "mug" close by, someone he could arrest if the theft went wrong. "… then I'm a hero, aren't I? I get a medal or something."

Perry learned of DI Robson's openness to a bribe when he was in the cells at a London magistrate's court, where he would be answering a charge of dishonestly handling 12 bottles of whisky. DS Harris told him he could keep from the magistrate full knowledge of Perry's long criminal record. In return, Perry would have to "give the Big Bloke a drink" when he got out of court. The Big Bloke was Harris's boss, Robson; "a drink" was slang for a bribe. The fee this time was £25 (£300 today). Robson's pay-off was on a higher scale, however – "oners", or a hundred pounds.

What emerged was a disturbing insight into a group of detectives milking a criminal for all they could get. It was being caught between these parasitic detectives that prompted Perry to talk to *The Times*. Not only was he being bled by Symonds and co – that was almost an accepted business expense for some London villains – but he faced the prospect of being framed for something he did not do or having to turn informer to keep the detectives off his back.

The taped conversation between DS Symonds and Perry drifted into the surreal when the detective started giving the criminal advice about how to manage his career in law-breaking. He started by telling Perry that when he made a lot of money on a job he should "poke it away". The sergeant said, "A lot of blokes I've known over the years blew it all on crumpet and booze, gambling and that, you know." Symonds advises that Perry invest his ill-gotten money in a little sweet shop, "keep a bird in there running it". Then if he did ever get caught, he would have a legit business to fall back on.

Symonds also told Perry to keep him informed of his criminal activities. The sergeant claimed this was so he could protect Perry by keeping straight detectives away from investigating his crimes. Symonds said he had useful contacts everywhere that he could call on. "I'm a little firm in a firm," Symonds explained. And later he said, "If you are nicked anywhere in London… I can get on the blower to someone in my firm who will know someone somewhere who can get something done. But out in the sticks they are all country coppers, aren't they? All old [fucking] swedes and that."

The sergeant continued in the role of agony aunt when Perry wanted to talk about the hundred-pound backhander DI Robson was demanding. Sitting in his black Wolseley saloon outside the Grove Tavern on Lordship Lane, Dulwich, Perry explained to Symonds that he was worried about a meeting he had been summoned to later that day with Robson at the Army and Navy Stores near Scotland Yard in Victoria. Perry had paid off the inspector and been told, "Now you've paid your £200 we're quits," Robson had told him. "What do you think we are, professional blackmailers?" Symonds, all heart, advised the thief to dodge this latest meeting if he had paid Robson everything he owed him. Robson, Symonds advised, might be planning to "fit up", or frame, Perry, "because we've got more villains in our game than you've got in yours, you know".

Perry's fears were realised when DI Robson confirmed that a professional blackmailer is exactly what he was. Robson demanded another £50 at their next rendezvous, at the Army and Navy Stores. If Perry did not pay up, the inspector said he would plant stolen goods on Perry and two of his associates during a forthcoming police raid.

Symonds, perhaps stating the bleeding obvious, counselled Perry about Robson's antics: "You've got to watch all this because otherwise you will be [fucking] skint all your life." Is it any wonder that, leeched on as he was by three greedy detectives, Perry went to the newspapers for help?

These allegations were explosive. Detailed accounts, much of it caught on tape, of Scotland Yard men demanding bribes, offering to "license" criminal operations, frame receivers and "mugs", and even help villains to avoid convictions were almost unheard of. And all of this printed in the staid, respectable *Times*.

There was no way the paper's news editor, Colin Webb, would have published such serious allegations without demanding strong corroboration. Perry's word alone was not good enough. His convictions included aiding an escape from a remand centre, actual bodily harm, theft and, most recently, handling the stolen whisky. Reporters Julian Mounter and Garry Lloyd certainly did not trust him and no jury would believe a word from him. They questioned him over and over again to test his claims. A sound engineer and photographer were assigned to assist the reporters in obtaining some neutral evidence in addition to Perry's account.

A microphone was put under the dashboard of Perry's car, with another inside his shirt. There were a number of mishaps, partly because the body mike was fairly primitive, but the dash recorder was excellent. Gradually, particularly when the team decided to use four recorders, the successful recordings and photos of meetings between Perry and the detectives were enough to add strength to the criminal's version of what was going on.

The investigation was conducted in total secrecy, with only *The Times*' editor being kept up to date. Perry was in constant fear that the detectives would hear of the tape recordings, but the subterfuge was never exposed. The tapes were transcribed immediately, the reporters' notes were typed up every day and statements were taken, signed and placed in a safe.

All of this is important because the investigation needed to be rigorous to withstand the hostility that would come its way from Scotland Yard following publication. Even Robert Mark was slightly disparaging about the journalists' efforts, saying such disclosures were rarely in the public interest or helpful to the process of justice. Officers often say the press should keep their noses out of such stories and leave real investigating to the police.

However, Mark did put his finger on the most crucial point here: "Why then did a newspaper with a worldwide reputation to sustain behave in this uncharacteristic manner?" he asked in his autobiography. "The answer was quite simple. The editor and his legal advisers did not believe that if the allegations against the detectives were disclosed privately to the Metropolitan Police they would be properly investigated." So, *The Times*' intervention had served a useful purpose – it rammed home the widespread feeling that the Met could not be trusted to scrupulously investigate its own people. It should also reduce a little of the resistance to Mark's forthcoming reforms.

The Times' journalists acknowledged they feared that, given the chance, Scotland Yard might try to hush up the story and it might never come out. When Robson and Harris came to trial, Garry Lloyd told the court, "During our inquiry we had knowledge that we were inquiring into 'a firm within a firm'. When you are dealing with a firm within a firm, you do not know who is the managing director."

What followed next confirmed their fears. *The Times* only told Scotland Yard of its allegations the night before publication when its tapes and documents were handed over to the Night Duty Officer. The Yard's top detective, Peter Brodie, Assistant Commissioner (Crime), was alerted. The police reaction, typical of an organisation more concerned with its reputation than rooting out alleged wrongdoing, was to investigate the journalists rather than the accounts of criminality among its detectives.

It is revealing to ask what action Scotland Yard would have taken if allegations of corruption had been levelled against a member of the public. It would have immediately investigated that person, of course. Whether the suspect had a criminal record or not, a warrant would have been obtained and their home and workplace searched. Diaries and papers would be examined, finances checked, associates interviewed. Normal police practice would be to respond with speed, before incriminating evidence could be destroyed.

From the moment *The Times'* allegations were published, however, Scotland Yard spent six days discussing what to do and questioning Michael Perry and the reporters. The best account of this affair is *The Fall of Scotland Yard*, written by Barry Cox, John Shirley and Martin Short, and published in 1977. In it they say, "The normal conduct of a criminal inquiry – searching the suspects' homes, desks, lockers – seems to have been totally neglected… The will of the CID to act promptly and firmly against the 'firm within a firm' did not seem to exist." Clearly, the reporters had been justified in not handing over their evidence before publication.

The force may have been angered to have been ambushed by the journalists. They may have felt loyalty to Robson, Harris and Symonds. They may also have been annoyed to have to conduct an inquiry in the full glare of publicity, which probably affected how they could carry it out. But it was still incumbent on them to thoroughly look into the possibility of law-breaking among their own.

They certainly put a lot of effort into interrogating the journalists. Lloyd and Mounter were questioned for eight hours a day over three weeks. The Yard also hired an expert to test the tapes to see whether they were forgeries. Of course, it would have been convenient if it could be proved that *The Times*' team had had the harebrained idea to invent the whole story, but even the most cynical detective must have thought that possibility pretty fanciful. The reporters also received threatening anonymous phone calls – "We'll get you for this" – and Mounter was followed on the London Underground on one occasion.

While obtaining statements was an essential part of such an inquiry, thoroughness was less evident when it came to taking disciplinary action against the three detectives under suspicion.

The Times' story had also referred to the activities of a senior officer who operated a system using scrap-metal dealers as middlemen. Scotland Yard had this man's name, but he was not suspended during the crucial open phase of the investigation. He would eventually be demoted, but he was allowed to carry on in a position of authority at his station, where evidence for the corruption inquiry was being collected.

The ruthless law-breaking and apparent attempts to defuse damage to the reputation of the police are both themes that are prominent in *Line of Duty*. Similar echoes are there of the efforts put in to sabotage the investigation into *The Times*' allegations.

The blatant cover-up effort that followed would have been admired by the OCG itself.

Types of corruption

Because corruption permeates every scene in *Line of Duty* and the events covered in this book, it is worth taking a moment to define this many-tentacled monster.

Most simply, corruption occurs when officers misuse their authority for personal profit or advantage, what is known as being bent for self. The other category is when they subvert the rules to gain a conviction that could not be achieved without infringing the law – bent for the job. Corruption can start with accepting a free coffee or meal and escalate from there.

Other infringements include fiddling expenses, padding overtime and using police vehicles for private journeys. Such cheats are in the "grass-eating" league of corruption.

At the more carnivorous end of the scale is the dodgy officer who accepts or demands money in exchange for not opposing bail or bringing any charges at all. Evidence might also be suppressed in return for a backhander. An officer on the make will take payment for protecting villains as they commit a crime. Then there is straightforward dishonesty – stealing from premises under police surveillance; pinching drugs, money or other goods seized from criminals; or taking a prisoner's property. This is all bent for self.

Straightforward theft is an obvious corrupt practice. A former senior officer told this author how this occurred in his experience. There would be suggestions that money was going missing, and members of a team would know that one or two of their number had a tendency for being light-fingered. If these officers saw money during the search of a property, they would lift it. The victim, being a suspected criminal, was often not in a position to report the theft. Rather than confront or report the suspected thieving officers, others on the team would never invite them on a search again. They would generally be given a wide berth by other detectives.

Another form of theft from criminals is the straightforward con. George Thomson-Smith, retired Met detective, outlined one scam. A suspect in police custody would be approached by a detective he may vaguely know and be told, "I could get you off this." He is told they need to pay off an officer in charge of the case. The suspect would arrange for a couple of grand to be handed over. He would then say to the detective working the case, "It's sorted, you've been paid." The officer in charge would reply to the stunned suspect, "What are you talking about? You're going to be charged." The realisation would hit the suspect – he had been ripped off by the first detective.

Another veteran of Scotland Yard in the 1960s and 70s, ex-Chief Superintendent Don Williams, a leading figure in A10, the real-life precursor to *Line of Duty*'s AC-12, tells the story of a pornographer who was facing trial. The pornographer told Williams he had asked the corrupt fixer, Detective Chief Superintendent Bill Moody, if he could influence the trial to help him. Williams recounts: "Moody said he wanted £15,000 cash. So the pornographer said, 'I went to my various bank accounts and I got the money. I put it in a Harrods bag, because we're going to meet at the Serpentine [lake in Hyde Park, which is near Harrods].' The pornographer handed over the money, but in the event the case was dropped for legal reasons."

Williams concludes, "So the bribe was paid for nothing. But [the pornographer] thought he was getting value for money. There was a lot of that sort of thing going on."

Inventing informants was another scam. Some corrupt officers developed close relationships with bent insurance loss adjustors. When stolen goods were recovered, the loss adjustor and the detective would invent an informant who had supposedly helped to locate the stolen goods. The detective and the insurance representative would then split the reward offered by the business from whom the goods were snatched, sometimes amounting to thousands of pounds.

In Series 2 of *Line of Duty*, Dot Cottan asks his close colleague Nigel Morton if he could "go the extra mile" for him. He wants Morton to give a false statement to the effect that dead detective Jeremy Cole was involved in the ambush of the police convoy.

This is a bid to implicate Cole as the criminal plant known as "the Caddy", deflecting attention away from Cottan, the actual Caddy. They later come to an arrangement whereby each agrees to cover for the other's nefarious activities. Officers covering up their colleagues' law-breaking is yet another type of corruption. It happened most noticeably during Scotland Yard's botched attempt to investigate widespread corruption uncovered by *The Times* in 1969, when DCS Bill Moody ensured the full scope of police criminality remained hidden from an investigation led by HM Inspector of Constabulary Frank Williamson (as we saw in chapter 2).

The offer of a bribe could be brazen for detectives during the 1970s. John O'Connor, a former commander, has said detectives all knew of such activity. "If you arrested a high-profile criminal, you very often got a phone call from another detective to say, 'Can anything be done?' What do you mean, can anything be done? It was asking you, can you water down the evidence? Can you accept a bribe? That's the way it would normally occur."

A majority of detectives were not members of the "firm within a firm". What was required for corruption to thrive, however, was for strategically placed officers in specific departments, including some senior figures, to be part of a shady network. Bosses could offer protection and cover for corrupt dealings in return for a share of the bribes.

Occasionally, an approach would be made to the wrong officer. The Albion pub at Ludgate Circus in London was once a meeting spot for criminals and detectives. One night in 1980 a punch-up between two well-dressed men broke out. One was Detective Superintendent John Keane and the other was Detective Inspector Bernard Gent. It started when Keane tried to wrestle a tape recorder he suspected Gent was using to tape a conversation in which he had offered Gent a £10,000 bribe.

This would be in return for Gent attempting to get a criminal contact of Keane's off a charge for a substantial robbery. Keane had apparently earlier phoned Gent to ask "if anything could be done". During the fist throwing, the pub's landlady shouted that if they did not stop, she would call the police. To which Gent replied, "We are the police." Keane was subsequently sentenced to three years for corruption.

In corruption terms, the flip side of helping a villain to avoid justice is framing him. Getting a confession illegally is the bent method for pushing a conviction forward. Officers might "verbal" or "gild the lily", which is to insert words into a suspect's statement to implicate him. This resulted in ludicrous statements being read out in court: "I did it. I cannot deny it. It's a fair cop, guv. You caught me bang to rights. I'm glad you came 'cause you stopped me doing something worse." Dialogue you would not find in the cheapest TV cop drama.

The existence of such practices was not acknowledged until well into the 1970s. Planting evidence on someone could also induce them to give in and confess. If browbeating did not make the suspect fold, then a straightforward beating would be used on occasion. These are examples of being bent for the job, justified in the past by an attitude expressed to author Peter Laurie in 1970: "If you went by the rules, the clear-up rate would be down from twenty-five per cent to two per cent."

Many of these methods were in play during Robert Mark's time. He said that policing when he was a young man in the 1940s was a "fairly rough and tough business". Questioning could be accompanied by threats of violence in the privacy of the police station. There were occasions, Mark says, when his hair stood on end as he witnessed the difference "between theory and practice in applying the rules governing police interrogation". He does not go into detail.

An attempt to tighten the rules of police conduct followed a notorious case from 1972. Maxwell Confait, aged 26, was murdered in a flat in Catford, south-east London. Three lads confessed to the murder and arson at the flat. These were Colin Lattimore, who was aged 18 but said to have a mental age of eight; Ronnie Leighton, 15; and Ahmet Salih, 14. All three were convicted of arson. Lattimore was found guilty of manslaughter on grounds of diminished responsibility, and Leighton of murder. Their appeals were dismissed. Then, three years later, the Court of Appeal quashed the convictions. It emerged that the boys had been kept without seeing a lawyer and with no parental contact, to endure hours of oppressive questioning before signing worthless confessions at two in the morning.

The response was the Police and Criminal Evidence Act 1984 – PACE. This replaced the Judges' Rules in a bid to stop the "fitting up" of suspects at police stations. It provided for legal representation, the tape recording of interviews – which are now very carefully depicted in *Line of Duty*'s much-loved interrogation scenes – and the length of detention without being charged. The following year, the Prosecution of Offences Act set up the Crown Prosecution Service. This ended much of the Met's role in prosecuting its own cases without qualified legal assistance. While police continued to gather evidence, the ending of their right to conduct their cases cut opportunities for corruption and bargaining power to induce suspects to plead guilty.

Racism is another form of corruption. In November 2021 the British Transport Police (BTP) apologised for "systemic racism" and the actions of a corrupt officer 50 years before in the 1970s. A BTP sergeant, Derek Ridgewell, lied in court at the trials of men including those who became known as the Waterloo Four, Oval Four and the Stockwell Six. To take one example, four young black men – Winston Trew, Sterling Christie, George

Griffiths and Constantine "Omar" Boucher – were arrested at Oval Tube station by Ridgewell's officers and went to court accused of assaulting a police officer and attempted theft. Trew has spoken of how he was punched in the head and body and forced to sign a confession. All four were sentenced to four years, later reduced to eight months. It was only in 2019 that the Court of Appeal finally overturned the convictions because of the unreliability of Ridgewell's evidence. BTP were warned of his criminal methods in 1973, but merely shifted him to a department investigating mailbag theft. There he got together with two criminals to split the proceeds from stolen mailbags. He died in jail of a heart attack in 1982 at the age of 37.

One justification for breaking the rules is that the law is stacked against detectives and favours criminals. The former commander John O'Connor explained on the BBC's 2021 documentary *Bent Coppers: Crossing the Line of Duty* that detective performance was measured by the number of arrests they made. "I have to say, if you were going to arrest a suspected person properly and within the law, you were going to have to be very, very patient." So there was pressure on detectives to sometimes bend the rules to make arrests, another example of "noble cause" corruption, or being "bent for the job".

We come back to the problem highlighted by Robert Mark as a cause of corruption – the detective having to meet and work alongside hardened criminals. The obvious danger is that this can end up with some officers getting too cosy and being tempted to cross the line.

Commander Ken Drury, head of the Flying Squad, came under suspicion in 1972 when the *Sunday People* revealed that he had been on holiday to Cyprus with one of Soho's biggest pornographers. He tried to explain away his associating with crooks like this: "If you have no association with the criminal fraternity, you don't know what is going on. It's no good going to the vicar's tea party and trying to gain information about organised teams of robbers."

Some aspects of police shadiness are subtle, and many are touched on in *Line of Duty*. In Series 1, Chief Superintendent Derek Hilton puts pressure on Hastings to simply pursue Tony Gates with lesser charges when AC-12 are trying to prove he was present at a murder scene. "There are only so many drains you can look down before AC-12 becomes a laughing stock," the slippery Hilton says. Turning a blind eye to such serious potential charges is clearly unethical.

In Series 4 Hilton puts huge pressure on Roz Huntley to charge the innocent, vulnerable Michael Farmer with murder. "There are facts and there is truth," he says to her with a Trumpian flourish. Orchestrating such wrongful convictions has occurred with a dispiriting regularity in real life – the cases of Maxwell Confait, the Birmingham Six, the Cardiff Three and many more – and must be the worst manifestation of bent for the job.

"I can't tell you how to run your department, but I want you to move Steve Arnott on," Gill Biggeloe tells Ted Hastings over dinner in Series 3. "Make him some other department's problem." This is after Lindsay Denton has compromised Arnott with the revelation during her interview that he had sexual contact with her. Again, moving an officer who has broken the rules, or is suspected of being bent, to another posting to "make him some other department's problem" is another form of corruption. Rather than bosses dealing with the troublemaker, they are allowing them to continue their villainous activities in some other department.

Of course, Biggeloe has an ulterior motive in wanting Arnott moved. She really wants to undermine AC-12's effectiveness.

But senior officers treating rotten colleagues like hot potatoes does happen in the real world. The result is some bent cops can be moved several times as those around them smell a rat, even on occasion getting promoted.

Ex-Met detectives will acknowledge that very few senior officers want to wash dirty laundry in public. They want to get rid of the problem without identifying it as an actual problem publicly. Some just do not want to draw attention to corruption within their command, so they decide the best thing to do is move it elsewhere.

Yet another police scam from this time involved mail-order pornography. Certain corrupt officers involved in policing the Soho porn trade during the early 1970s saw that big sums were being made from mail-order porn. Former detective Don Williams, who spent much of his career hunting bent officers, explains, "The coppers got onto this. They thought, *We can do this*. And they put an advert out and they got the money in and they never sent the books. But people didn't complain. If you've sent off for a dirty book and you've spent a tenner, you think, *It was my fault*. So they [corrupt officers] made a lot of money doing this. They were making big bloody money."

Then there is the difficult and hidden area of Masonic membership. Real-world concerns about the ways in which membership of the secret brotherhood can compromise the integrity and effectiveness of officers are also reflected in *Line of Duty*. The problem with Freemasonry in the police is that it is a clandestine network, arousing suspicions of a lack of openness and accountability among serving officers who are members. If a male officer is promoted at work (most lodges exclude women), is that because he is the best person for the role, or because he and the person making the appointment are Masons? Are officers in the same lodge, or branch, as criminals they might have to investigate?

Suspicions of favouritism and divided loyalties have always dogged the police as a result of the Masonic brotherhood within its ranks. One detective told this author that whenever a colleague considered to be "useless" got promoted, it was easy to wonder if they had got a leg up from Masonic mates.

Jackie Malton, the Flying Squad detective who became the role model for Jane Tennison in Lynda La Plante's *Prime Suspect*, said recently in her autobiography that she saw a photo of a lodge inauguration and recognised two-thirds of the 60 or so men present. Most were senior officers. A male colleague who previously turned down an invitation to join the Masons told her he was warned that not being a Freemason would harm his career.

Steve Arnott in Series 3 realises that his boss, Ted Hastings, is a Freemason when he sees the Masonic handshake between Hastings and former Chief Superintendent Patrick Fairbank. Fairbank, suspected of being part of a paedophile ring, surprises Arnott and Kate Fleming when they try to interview him at his home. Unknown to them, he has summoned Hastings to join them at the interview, and it is clear Fairbank expects his fellow Mason to keep his name out of the investigation. Suddenly, Arnott and Fleming are not sure they can trust their boss to sanction a thorough probe into Fairbank's past. Later in the episode, when Fleming seeks the go-ahead to conduct an undercover operation, it is to a female senior officer that she goes for permission rather than Hastings. This is because, with women largely excluded from the secret male network of mutual favours and advancements, there is little chance the female officer will leak knowledge of her undercover role to Fairbank or his allies. In the end, Hastings puts duty above the Masonic code and arrests Fairbank.

It is hard to justify being a police officer and a member of a secret society that promotes mutual self-advancement. Police officers are expected to be transparent, so the public do not have to wonder whether they have, for example, risen the ranks because their Masonic chums secured promotions for them. And crucially, following the scandals from the 1960s to the 1980s, when it emerged that a few officers were in the same Masonic lodges as career criminals, there should be no concerns that a detective would swing an investigation in a villain's favour because they had a Masonic allegiance to them.

The way this might work was shown in the 1999 case of former detective and Freemason Duncan Hanrahan. He was sent down for more than eight years for conspiracy to rob, supply drugs and pervert the course of justice. It was revealed during his Old Bailey trial that he had contacted a fellow Freemason and serving officer, asking to be put in touch with another officer. Hanrahan, by this time working as a private detective, then tried to bribe that officer to destroy evidence in another case. On this occasion, abuse of the Masonic ties failed when the serving officer reported Hanrahan's approach, but it is easy to see that the potential for murky associations remains.

Brian (now Lord) Paddick, former Deputy Assistant Commissioner, recounts in his autobiography, *Line of Fire*, how he joined the Masons as a 21-year-old officer. He was serving under an unpopular superintendent in West London and one day asked the man if he was "on the square" (the square and compasses being the symbol of Freemasonry), meaning, are you a Freemason? In an instant the superintendent's attitude to him changed, "suddenly he became my best friend". He was taken aback by this abrupt friendliness but says it "was not the last time someone's attitude to me was to change instantly when he discovered my Masonic links".

Brian Hilliard, former editor of *Police Review*, found during his research into a book on the Flying Squad that every member of the squad during the 1960s was almost certainly a Freemason. Just about every CID man he spoke to at that time was one.

Commissioner after commissioner – Sir Kenneth Newman, Lord Imbert, Lord Condon, Bernard Hogan-Howe – have all voiced opposition to membership of the society for police officers. But as recently as 2017, Steve White, retiring chair of the Police Federation, which represents rank-and-file officers, was still complaining about Freemasonry. He and his colleagues suspected there were pockets of Masons who were blocking the progress of women and black and ethnic minority communities. The Masons denied any conflict of interest and argued that they are a social group encouraging self-improvement.

Despite the conflict of interest, the Masons continue in the police. Which is why *Line of Duty*, as ever with its finger on the pulse of real events, has featured storylines about it.

There is one final area that has raised concerns in the past. This occurs when detectives endeavour to stonewall, delay, deflect and generally sabotage official inquiries into alleged police venality. Every *Line of Duty* series features efforts deployed by corrupt officers to evade AC-12 by using delay and obfuscation.

In Series 1, DCI Tony Gates deletes a missing-person report implicating his lover, Jackie Laverty, in the killing of her accountant. DI Dot Cottan tries a cruder tactic in Series 3 when he attempts to deflect AC-12 attention away from himself by suggesting Steve Arnott planted £50,000 on Lindsay Denton.

On a bigger scale, Series 4 sees ACC Derek Hilton – who we later discover is under the thumb of the Organised Crime Group – telling Ted Hastings that his AC-12 team is ineffectual and corrupt. This is a classic case of deflecting attention from your criminal masters by discrediting the investigators.

In the real world the most potent example of this kind of spoiling tactic would be the shocking case of the murder of private investigator Daniel Morgan. He was found in the car park of a south London pub, the Golden Lion in Sydenham, in 1987, having been killed with an axe. Scotland Yard has apologised and acknowledged that police corruption hampered the original efforts to gather vital evidence. In the ensuing 36 years there have been six major probes into the scandal, the most recent being the Independent Panel, which in 2021 branded the Met institutionally corrupt. Its investigation was expected to take a couple of years, but it actually dragged on for almost eight years, partly because the Met took so long to hand over information.

If ever a cabal of corrupt officers existed that wanted to hide the truth about a controversial case, then perpetuating a decades-long spin cycle of reports and investigations must be an effective way to do it.

On a smaller scale, there is the poorly conducted investigation, what one officer told this author was known as a "light-touch" investigation. This occurred when someone in authority wanted an allegation to go away or fizzle out. The detective given such a task would make that happen by only speaking to people they knew would not be able to help the inquiry, not corroborating certain details, or saying they are too difficult to confirm. All of this would lead to a recommendation that there was not enough evidence to justify a full investigation or prosecution.

A closer look at the dirty tricks deployed during the police investigation into the 1969 *Times* corruption allegations gives a flavour of how this might work.

The reality confirms that *Line of Duty* is often closer to the truth than audiences may realise.

An investigation sabotaged by corrupt detectives

At the climax of Series 5 of *Line of Duty*, Gill Biggeloe makes her speech to Ted Hastings about the importance of PR – public relations, or ensuring the police maintain an image of integrity. The implication is that it is better that some suspected corrupt officers should not be investigated in order to protect the force's image.

Biggeloe, we discover later, has her own toxic agenda and is out to destroy the superintendent. But with this brazenly cynical speech – anti-corruption as a branch of public relations – she reveals her hidden agenda, one that is sometimes levelled against real police forces. This is that wrongdoing by officers needs to be played down and the reputation of the force must be protected at all costs.

As we have seen, the early days of the investigation into *The Times*' revelations got off to a ponderous, less-than-convincing start, appearing to be more of an investigation of the journalists than the allegations they put forward.

But with the appointment of Frank Williamson, an investigation was finally moving forward. However, Williamson, who was HM Inspector of Constabulary, did not have the power to really delve into the protected nooks of the Met. What was really needed was a senior chief constable with full powers to conduct the investigation, assisted by a special team of Met and provincial officers. Williamson, on the other hand, was appointed to "advise" the inquiry. He was not in control.

Instead, once again, the Met was allowed to investigate itself, with Frank Williamson overseeing inquiries. While Williamson was tenacious and passionate about combating corruption, he soon realised he faced an uphill slog. As previously noted, vital time was lost after *The Times* went to press with its bombshell. Six days were frittered away discussing the issue and getting statements from *The Times*' reporters. This should have happened in tandem with gathering evidence on the detectives cited in the articles. Instead, days during which statements could have been taken and searches made were wasted.

Finally, after six days, DI Bernard Robson, DS Gordon Harris and DS John Symonds were suspended. Williamson came in on 9 December. Like Mark, he thought an independent inquiry should have been set up, and was well aware of how damaging Scotland Yard's foot-dragging had probably been. On his appointment, he also warned the Home Secretary, James Callaghan, "Well, if they were going to do any damage, they'll have done it. Papers and records will have been destroyed…" One of his first discoveries was indeed that important documents had already gone missing, while the suspended officers' diaries and notebooks had not even been collected. Some vital documents were never found.

Williamson gathered a team of trusted provincial officers to assist him, but one Deputy Assistant Commissioner told him he would not allow anyone from outside the Met to investigate its members. The Met old guard was closing ranks. Williamson's men were only allowed to question other provincial officers. The geographic spread of the inquiries included the Home Counties because Robson and Harris had been looking into organised thieves committing crimes across the region.

Representing the Met on the inquiry was Detective Chief Superintendent Fred Lambert. Ominously, another chief superintendent, Bill Moody, one of the Yard's most corrupt men, was inserted alongside Lambert. Moody would end up in jail a few years later, but whether there were doubts about him at the Yard during this time or not, his involvement seems suspicious and would become more so.

Despite run-ins with the Yard hierarchy, Williamson's team located other hardened thieves who had similar stories about

DS Symonds to Michael Perry's bribery allegations in *The Times*. One, Douglas MacDonald, said that while he had absconded from home leave from Lewes Prison for crimes including stealing and assaulting a policeman, he had paid Symonds for a licence to stay out, during which time he committed more crimes. MacDonald admitted to taking part in 19 shop raids using duplicate keys. Individually, such accounts could be deemed questionable, but together they were adding a fuller picture of Symonds' energetic criminal dealings.

Despite such victories for Williamson and Lambert, they soon encountered another internal problem. Office security for their team was poor. At one point the "Action Book", a record of tasks given to investigating detectives, was taken and never recovered. Williamson moved the operation from Scotland Yard to Tintagel House, an office block by the Thames at Vauxhall. He and Lambert began to work closely, and Williamson had probably grown to trust Lambert. However, to add to Williamson's frustration, his provincial detectives were digging up a lot of new leads on corruption, while the Scotland Yard men found little beyond what *The Times* had already uncovered.

One incident was a good example of the Met's low-powered inquiry. A Peckham thief called Daniel Crouch, under questioning by Williamson's men, asserted that a police motorbike cop had issued him with a traffic ticket. Crouch gave the time and place where this happened. He then claimed he had paid DS Symonds £15 to intercept the ticket and get rid of it. It was important that Williamson's detectives verified such claims, as it was unlikely a jury would accept such uncorroborated testimony from a villain. The task of tracing the motorcycle cop should have been straightforward because of the details Crouch gave. It was given to a Met chief inspector who, after three weeks, had still not found the motorcycle officer in his own city. Frustrated, Williamson put one of his sergeants on the job. The sergeant found the officer within two hours and Crouch's story checked out. This is just one incident, but it was an example of why forces outside London often did not trust the Met. It is also another example of the aforementioned tactic of a "light touch" investigation.

A serious blow then hit Williamson's inquiry. In May 1970, DCS (Detective Chief Superintendent Fred Lambert) Lambert was removed from the team, with DCS Moody – a major-league bent officer – taking his place. If the Scotland Yard bigwigs did not realise that Moody was highly suspect, it did not take long for Williamson to see through the chief superintendent who would be working alongside him.

It seems unlikely to have been a coincidence that just when Lambert, representing the Met, and Williamson's provincial investigators were making good progress that Lambert should be kicked into touch. Moreover, when there were some 30 detective chief superintendents at Scotland Yard to choose from, it is odd that it should be a seriously corrupt officer with a lot to lose who was parachuted into the inquiry. At this time, Moody was head of the Obscene Publications Squad, which was mired in Soho criminality. He and a network of detectives were being paid by crooks for unofficial permission to open porn shops selling illegal material.

Lambert was due to interview a man called Frankie Holbert, a middleman between the porn merchants and Moody's bent officers, in connection with *The Times*' allegations. There was a risk that Holbert, or Little Frankie as he was known, would reveal his role in Moody's criminal operation. First, Moody appropriated the area of the inquiry that involved Holbert. Later, in May, he took over completely. What better way to ensure Moody's corrupt set-up was kept secret and the corruption scandal did not spread from Robson-Harris-Symonds to the far more serious racket in Soho? Whether Moody pushed to get involved in Williamson's probe or he was placed there by others in the Met to limit the true scale of corruption is not known. It seems he never got round to interviewing Holbert. But such a sabotage operation would not look out of place in the world of AC-12.

The axing of Lambert was abrupt and brutal. The sequence of events started when he told Moody he was just finishing a 70-page report on the inquiry. Moody offered to read it and help complete it. Lambert agreed. Almost immediately, Dick Chitty, Deputy Assistant Commissioner, appeared in Lambert's office. A big argument followed about the conduct of the inquiry. Lambert threatened to throw the DAC out of his office. Chitty left, but soon after, Commander Wally Virgo, Lambert's immediate boss as head of C1 (serious crimes), turned up. Virgo told Lambert he was off *The Times*' investigation. "You have backed the wrong horse," Virgo said. "You have backed Frank Williamson against your own senior officers." Scotland Yard's instinctive objective to block outsiders from examining its internal affairs was alive and well. Lambert's reward for cooperating with Williamson was to be assigned to deal with Virgo's mail. From investigator to clerk. Virgo soon moved him to another dead-end job, liaison with Interpol. He went on permanent sick leave in September 1970 and left the Met in early 1971. Lambert seems a text-book example of how to sideline and drive out a colleague who is "not one of us".

This sequence of events could have been a blueprint for the moment in *Line of Duty*'s Series 6, in which DCC Andrea Wise pushes Ted Hastings out of AC-12 into retirement. Her move also came as Hastings' team was getting close to exposing major police corruption.

In 1977 there were further twists to Lambert's demise. Moody and Virgo were on trial for accepting bribes, and in court, Virgo tried to trash Lambert's reputation. He was, Virgo suggested, a drunk, incompetent and unfit for the job. Virgo could produce no written reports or memos that he had made at the time to back up his claims in court of Lambert's inadequacies. Assistant Commissioner Peter Brodie gave a variation on this theme – Lambert had been sidelined because Frank Williamson said he had slowed down the investigation. Brodie had decided that Lambert was not up to the job after being told by others – Virgo and Chitty – that he had domestic problems that were distracting him. Had Brodie ever asked Lambert about these domestic issues? No, he had taken the word of Virgo and Chitty. However, Williamson rejected the attacks on Lambert when he gave evidence. He said Lambert was competent and impartial. Williamson also rejected the brazen suggestion that it was he who had requested that Moody replace Lambert.

The treatment of Lambert reveals how the probe into CID conduct was undermined. Lambert was doing a good, if unpopular, job in working alongside Williamson to establish whether *The Times'* revelations were true. As a result, he was abruptly shunted aside into ignominious roles, effectively prompting him to leave the force. For good measure, his reputation was trashed to completely discredit anything he could say later about the investigation. Lambert rejected Virgo's claims.

Williamson's efforts also ended in bitterness and frustration. Chitty relieved Moody of his duties with the Obscene Publications Squad so that he could devote all his dubious attention to *The Times'* allegations. He and Williamson had to share an office at Tintagel House and the two men were like repelling magnets.

Williamson, aged 52, former Chief Constable of Cumbria, looked like a humourless accountant. He was, however, a dedicated former detective, devoted to rooting out criminal officers. As Her Majesty's Inspector of Constabulary, his job was to independently assess police performance, but he no longer had police powers. This put him at a disadvantage in regard to his supposed partner, Moody. The chief superintendent quickly rubbed Williamson up the wrong way with his flash-Harry lifestyle. A car park incident at Tintagel House perfectly summed up the culture clash between them. Where Williamson drove a sober Austin 1800, Moody sped around in a 2.5-litre Triumph and a 1.5-litre Lancia. Moody walked over to Williamson in the car park and, indicating his Austin, said, "Is that the best you can do?" Williamson would say later, "In fact, that was the best I could do." And of Moody he would say, "I was worried about his lifestyle. I was worried about his personal conduct and attitude. I was certainly worried about his motor cars."

Where Williamson disapproved of any relationship with villains that might inhibit their effectiveness as law enforcers, Moody drank and socialised with them, effectively trying to be their mate to disarm them (though in his case he became one of them). Moody's offers of hospitality were routinely turned down by Williamson, who came to suspect these might have been an effort to compromise him. The scale of his socialising certainly stunned Williamson. On one occasion, Moody entertained the whole investigation team and their wives at a party that would have cost a lot of money.

While it was Brodie who had been prompted into removing Fred Lambert, Williamson would later reveal it was Chief Superintendent John du Rose, another leading figure in the Scotland Yard hierarchy, who foisted Moody on the inquiry. Williamson said of him, "Du Rose and I fell out on the very first day I was there. He came into the office and said, 'I don't know what you're doing here.'" If he was under any illusion the Met did not want him, Williamson soon discovered that the Commissioner, Sir John Waldron, and Brodie, Assistant Commissioner, offered him no backing whatsoever. "They shut the door completely on me." Williamson also said Brodie accused him of being dishonest in the officers' mess as part of a campaign of vilification against him.

Moody turned out to be a whirlwind of activity, giving the appearance of throwing himself into the inquiry. And yet, some of those he investigated did not need to be looked at, while those who did were not made to reveal anything that could lead to a criminal charge. Again, it is the time-dishonoured tactic of conducting a "light investigation", designed to get nowhere. In the end, DI Robson and DS Harris were convicted on evidence largely amassed by *The Times*' reporters. DS Symonds was the only other detective charged. Robson and Harris were tried in January 1972. They were found guilty, with Harris getting six years and Robson a total of seven. The charges included conspiracy to demand money with menaces and conspiracy to pervert the course of justice.

Williamson may have been sure the corruption spread much further than Harris, Robson and Symonds, and during his testimony Perry asserted that he bribed five officers, including the two in the dock. But *The Times* had not collected evidence against the other three, so if Perry was telling the truth, they got away with it. However, with Moody guiding the Met's investigation, the only wrongdoers convicted were the two men against whom *The Times* had been able to offer evidence.

They appealed but it was turned down. Here the judge, Lord Justice Edmond Davies, paid tribute to *The Times* journalists: "It would be churlish were we to fail to make mention of the great public service rendered by these two reporters. It was, it would appear, mainly their intrepidity and skill which laid bare a hideous cancer…" Intrepidity and skill, Williamson probably felt, were what had been missing from Moody's efforts. It was clear these had been directed at keeping a lid on Williamson's team and ensuring no other detectives beyond Robson and Harris were charged.

So, what of Symonds, the detective who had talked of a firm within a firm? His trial was due to start at the Old Bailey on 12 April 1972. However, he was nowhere to be found. He had skipped the country during the Robson–Harris trial. You might have thought that the police would be alive to this possibility and would have asked that his passport be confiscated, or have checked whether he was selling his property, buying a mobile caravan and purchasing tickets to go abroad. Alas, none of this was done. Of course, with his disappearance, another embarrassing trial for the Met was averted.

Events behind his disappearance were disturbing. Symonds had argued against going on trial with Robson and Harris and he had threatened to reveal more serious corruption going on. He wrote down the names of more than one hundred corrupt officers, along with many other details. He could stand up in court and blurt the whole lot out. Moody, who Symonds knew well, told him they would not let him go on trial. He offered Symonds some money to get out of the country. Speaking in 1998, Symonds revealed, "Moody and co gave me £2,000 to go abroad and I was promised more, which never came. They just wanted me out the way." He returned to Britain in 1981, after nine years on the run, and got two years for corruption.

It was job done for Moody, who had ensured that his corrupt network was safe for now and that only the two rotten apples, Robson and Harris – who were sunk by *The Times* anyway – were sacrificed.

Line of Duty's Gill Biggeloe, who, as we have seen, asserted that the series' Central Police needed to find just enough bent coppers to avoid accusations of a cover-up, would have approved.

Frank Williamson retired, defeated. He always felt that if he had had another 20 good investigators at his side, he could have built a case against many of the 30-odd officers mentioned in *The Times'* report. He was clear later who his chief antagonists had been: "Moody was clearly sent into that inquiry to sabotage it. Du Rose was active in the obstruction of *The Times* inquiry right from the word go." Robert Mark, not yet in the commissioner's chair, had been watching all this closely. When his chance came, he would not let any Brodies or Moodys give him the runaround.

Meanwhile, Moody, his boss Commander Wally Virgo and other members of the firm may have thought they were in the clear. However, a bigger danger was lurking just around the corner.

4 – 'People choked on their cornflakes' – further revelations

'I didn't float up the Lagan in a bubble'

Events surrounding *The Times'* revelations reveal the lengths that certain senior Met officers would take to derail an investigation into their own ranks. Destroying the reputations of fellow colleagues, allowing bent officers to avoid justice and covering up evidence were some of the tactics used.

Many officers of integrity have fallen to such dirty practices down the years. It is because *Line of Duty* is so near the knuckle that reflections of such real-life treacheries filter into the drama. Dot Cottan attempts to deflect scrutiny from himself by trying to frame Steve Arnott as being "the Caddy" in Series 3. Series 4 shows Detective Chief Inspector Roz Huntley misdirecting a murder investigation in several ways to deflect from her own guilt. Having killed Forensic Coordinator Tim Ifield, she breaks a multitude of laws to tamper with forensic evidence and implicate several innocent people in the killing of Ifield and other victims.

And just as Fred Lambert was pressured to leave the Met, so a whole squad of characters has put in a diligent shift to stop Ted Hastings from uncovering a high-level network of bent officers in Central Police, and finally to push the superintendent out of policing altogether. Step forward lawyer Gill Biggeloe and senior officers Derek Hilton, Philip Osborne and Andrea Wise – all have insisted AC-12 was chasing phantoms trying to prove the Organised Crime Group had several top cops under its thumb.

Now as we look at the scale of corruption in 1972 confronting Hastings' real-life equivalent, Robert Mark, we hit the premier league of criminality for that time.

A couple of months before Mark took over as Commissioner on 17 April 1972, the *Sunday People* had published another wrecking ball of a story about bent coppers.

This was the previously mentioned outrageous account of how the Commander of the Flying Squad, Ken Drury, had been on holiday in Cyprus with one of Soho's biggest porn merchants, Jimmy Humphreys. The two men were even joined on the sunny jaunt by their wives.

Humphreys, after a few spells in prison, had opened a strip club in Old Compton Street during the 1960s, where Rusty, his wife, performed. The couple were later partners in a successful strip club on Walker's Court, an alley between Brewer Street and Berwick Street. Well turned out and quite personable, Humphreys got to know Soho's major players, such as Bernie Silver, and his profitable successes, with Rusty as business partner, saw him expand into other properties in the "naughty square mile".

By 1969 Humphreys could see that there were huge profits to be made in selling pornography in Soho. As journalist and author Martin Short put it, "Soho, in terms of pornography, was a huge corruption machine in which hundreds of thousands of pounds were being paid every year to crooked cops from a business which was making millions."

Humphreys owned many Soho properties and had lots of criminal contacts. But he lacked one vital bridge into the porn trade – contacts in the Metropolitan Police, specifically the Obscene Publications Squad. To meet the right detective,

Humphreys needed, ironically enough, the help of another criminal.

The man at the centre of the Soho web was the aforementioned Bernie Silver, who ran a network of flats for prostitution across the West End, as well as clip joints and dirty-book shops. Silver was a Soho kingpin because he was paying senior detectives for "protection", effectively an unofficial licence to run sex and porn businesses. Eventually, Commander Wally Virgo, the man who did so much to wreck Fred Lambert's police career, asked Silver to arrange an introduction between Humphreys and the head of the Obscene Publications Squad, Detective Chief Superintendent Bill Moody. Moody would sell Humphreys a licence – effectively give his permission to run his porn-mag outlet – and Silver would share in his profits in return for the introduction. Moody was effectively running the biggest gang in Soho. Humphreys would later say he paid £14,000 to open his magazine shop in Rupert Street (around £155,000 in today's money), and that was just to open the shop. He also had to pay a weekly kickback of £2,000 (£22,000). "We were partners in business," Humphreys said. "You can't feel any more secure than having Scotland Yard telling you you can operate. It was a licence to print money."

Former Chief Superintendent Don Williams, a leading member of Robert Mark's new anti-corruption squad A10, remembers Bill Moody well: "Bill Moody, well-named Wicked Bill Moody, because he was a wicked bastard." He went into the Porn Squad where he organised the collection of bribes efficiently and ruthlessly. "Until his day it was just hit or miss," Williams told this author. "But when Bill Moody took over, it was professionally organised. Anybody working in porn was obliged to pay a fee. He was paid for this, and there was a share-out on a Friday afternoon in the porn office."

Moody used some of his officers as go-betweens and bribe collectors, making rounds between porn operators. His boss, Commander Virgo, took a cut of the haul. While it was a minority of CID officers that were involved in the racket, on the other hand, if it reached to the level of commander, there was obviously a significant hierarchy of corruption underneath him. And, of course, there was no scrutiny of their activities from any officers outside of the Met.

In 1967 there had been 28 sex-book shops in Soho, which had always been a notorious quarter of nightclubs, prostitution, criminal hang-outs and strip clubs. By 1970 the number of porn stores had more than doubled, thanks to demand, a more tolerant climate and bent police. The hard-core material, which could be judged to "deprave and corrupt" in the language of the Obscene Publications Act, was hidden in a backroom of the shops for customers who showed an interest. The porn stock was part of the deal with Moody's men. So, when Commander Virgo would issue a warrant for a shop to be raided, the owner would be warned to close or remove the hard-core stuff. A sham raid would then go ahead. Some magazines would be confiscated, but the porn operator could pay a fee and collect his material from the storeroom at Holborn police station.

Rusty Humphreys would describe "bung day" – when detectives were paid off – as being like "Union Station", with people coming and going. Hundreds in cash were exchanged, along with jewellery, silverware, coats, bracelets. With porn generating so much money, it was not long before people became greedy.

Jimmy Humphreys gave an insight into the friction among the detectives. As Wally Virgo was a top London Met commander, Humphreys was careful to ensure he was looked after. So, when Virgo asked Humphreys – behind Moody's back – for a list of all the Soho shops and how much they were paying each week to Moody, Humphreys explained what happened next: "I gave him the list. He grabbed my hand and said, 'Jimmy, you must help me. I'm being fucked for my whack.' This is the top bloody commander in London. I thought, *Christ, I can't believe it.* You see what money does to people." A Soho criminal shaking his head at the avarice of bent cops.

Holidaying with a vice king

Commander Ken Drury, meanwhile, was head of the Flying Squad and third wheel in the set-up. Humphreys said he paid Drury £100 a week (£1,100 approximately today) to keep Flying Squad detectives away from his shops. On top of this, Humphreys was lavish with hospitality, taking Drury several times a week to dinners and lunches, giving him presents for his wife.

Drury, who swaggered around and was loud – he was known as "Trumpet" – became quite hefty under the onslaught of rich eating and drinking provided by the porn merchant. So close did the two become that Humphreys did not apparently give offence when he bought a course of slimming pills and a rowing machine for "Trumpet". In fact, Drury was so into Humphreys' largesse that he thought nothing of taking his wife to join him and Rusty on the holiday to Cyprus.

Drury had literally grown fat on the proceeds of corruption, and, like other detectives on the take, had also grown arrogant enough to think he would never be exposed. Enter the *Sunday People*. Thinking there might be a good story in the porn trade flourishing in Soho, they sent reporters to the sex shops to chat to their front men. They picked up several complaints about having to pay the police so much. But one reporter heard what he might have thought was an outlandish story that Drury had even been on holiday with Jimmy Humphreys.

The crucial question for the *People* reporters was this: who was it that paid for the trip? If it was Scotland Yard, then it might be deemed an official journey. If it was a private holiday, who paid? A reporter was sent to Cyprus and found the quartet had been on a package tour from Cook's. The newspaper was delighted when Cook's was able to produce the bill of £513 for it (£5,000 today) – paid by "Mr J Humphreys". Laurie Manifold, the *People's* assistant editor, said, "The whole thing was corrupt, without any doubt."

"Police Chief and the Porn King" was the front-page story that followed. This sensational report not only implicated Ken Drury but also highlighted the venal ties between pornographers and the detectives. "This was a double-whammy," was how author Martin Short summed it up. "Absolutely, people choked on their cornflakes that Sunday morning." The allegations were far more devastating than those of *The Times* just over two years earlier.

Drury's response? He was in Cyprus searching for Ronnie Biggs, one of the gang who committed the Great Train Robbery of 1963 and was still on the run. Humphreys had been helping him. Humphreys, clearly wanting to keep in with Drury, backed him up in this flimsy yarn. Until recently, Met protocol would see Scotland Yard closing ranks around Drury. And, indeed, CID argued that to suspend Drury, who had received 23 commendations in a 36-year career, would undermine morale, encourage villains and damage the reputation of the force.

This time, however, CID were dealing with Robert Mark, whose response was, "Tell me the old, old story… My reply was that failure to suspend would confirm the public's worst suspicions and, whatever the outcome, was inevitable." The *People's* bombshell was published on 27 February 1972, a few weeks before Mark was due to replace Sir John Waldron as Commissioner. However, at this point, he was Commissioner

Designate, effectively now the most powerful voice in Scotland Yard. The battle over Drury's suspension led to Mark's final trial of strength with C department, which encompassed CID and was run by Assistant Commissioner Peter Brodie. "This time," Mark later wrote, "as commissioner designate, I was not prepared to stand any nonsense and took such action as to leave the commissioner no choice but to suspend." There would be no cosy cover-up here.

Drury told the media, "I'm most surprised that I've been suspended. In fact, I'd go so far as to say I'm amazed that I've been suspended." He no doubt was taken aback. Detectives facing such allegations were usually allowed to carry on as if nothing had happened. Under the new Commissioner, Drury was so far out in the cold that later on Mark would not even give him a reference.

Brodie, Mark's longstanding antagonist, stood down due to ill health shortly after Drury's suspension, though it is likely Mark would have shuffled him to a different post if he had not left the force. It has been asked whether Brodie, who had backed Lambert's removal and supported Moody, was another corrupt senior officer. Mark says not, that Brodie's problem was that he was too trusting, could not accept anyone around him was tainted by criminality. His solidarity whenever the conduct of detectives was questioned showed that his loyalties could be misguided. Frank Williamson, whose investigation into *The Times*' revelations was curtailed by Moody and who was badly treated by Brodie, was more blunt: "I would love to be able to tell you that Brodie was bent because it would be retribution. I cannot... but I can tell you this: he was completely and utterly stupid."

Drury also seemed to have mislaid his intelligence when he made his next move. Having talked Humphreys into lying to the

News of the World with the credulity-stretching story about their having been on the lookout for Ronnie Biggs by the Med, he then sold his own version of events to the same paper. Having been served with disciplinary papers in April and having resigned from the force on 1 May, Drury then told the *News of the World* that Humphreys and his wife had actually been his informers.

Being labelled a grass or police informer is never good for the health or business prospects of anyone who mixes with criminals. Humphreys and his wife were infuriated by Drury's unthinking comments. Humphreys, who up to this time tried to avoid publicity, now called a press conference at his Soho offices. The Biggs angle was all lies, he told the pressmen. He, Drury and their wives were on holiday, which Humphreys had paid for. Drury had once been respected as head of the Flying Squad, but his reputation was badly damaged after this.

It was then Humphreys' turn to make a mistake and harm his own position. His wife's ex-lover, a man called Peter Garfath, and Humphreys, who was accompanied by around six other men, got involved in a knife fight in the lavatory of Marylebone's Dauphine Club. This saw Garfath get slashed across the face. While Humphreys fled to Holland, Rusty was arrested and charged with conspiracy to pervert the course of justice and conspiracy to cause grievous bodily harm to Garfath (she was later acquitted). In custody, she complained to Mark's new A10 anti-corruption team about certain senior detectives and their corrupt dealings with her husband.

One of Mark's hand-picked new squad of trusted officers was given the job of looking into Rusty's claims, which she said were recorded in her husband's diaries. These had been taken by the Serious Crime Squad from the couple's Soho flat after her arrest. Deputy Assistant Commissioner Gilbert Kelland was asked to look into Rusty's complaint. Having been stationed in the West End for many years, he had long felt that the policing of the Soho porn trade should be taken away from the Obscene Publications Squad and given to uniformed officers – a view that chimed with Robert Mark. Dealing with Mrs Humphreys' complaint would now balloon into a major probe into what was known as the Dirty Squad of officers.

Kelland had joined the Met as a constable in 1946. He had competed as a distance runner for the force, risen through the ranks and had experience dealing with vice in the West End. In 1952, as a trainee inspector at the National Police College, the candidates were asked to write a thesis, and Kelland chose as his subject police corruption. The superintendent in charge told him there was insufficient written material on that and suggested writing about policing crowds instead. "What a pity," Kelland wrote later, "there was such a taboo on open discussion about the problem of corruption at that period, especially among officers being prepared for middle and senior management positions." More openness on the subject might have prevented much damage to the police service later on, he argued.

At first, Kelland had his doubts about Rusty's explosive assertion that her husband's diaries for 1971 and 1972 contained detailed accounts of his dealings with bent detectives. If they did, these should have immediately come to light when the Serious Crime Squad took possession of them three months previously. So, why had nothing been heard about these potentially vital diaries since then? "The explanation that was given for this oversight," Kelland explained in his book *Crime in London*, "was the pressure of work on the senior officers of the squad dealing with her case, but I have always found this difficult to accept."

He demanded to see Humphreys' diaries himself. Kelland found they identified 21 detectives that were Humphreys' contacts, ranking from detective inspector to commander. They included the home and office phone numbers of senior officers. Humphreys also mentioned his dealings with porn associates, such as Bernie Silver. Kelland's next job was to corroborate the appointments and relationships indicated, but there was no doubt that the diaries opened major lines of inquiry.

Kelland's rejection of the excuse that the Serious Crime Squad had been too busy to look at the diaries appears justified. Despite Robert Mark's efforts to combat entrenched corruption and indifference to it, it would seem there were still elements at Scotland Yard that preferred the foot-dragging approach to investigating their own colleagues in CID.

As he dug into this venal network, Kelland found another instance of shoddy investigation. In 1971, a year before its revelations about Drury and Humphreys jetting off to the sun, the *Sunday People* had run another exposé about the Soho porn industry. It named the major players – Jeff Phillips, Gerry Citron, John Mason, Frank Mifsud, Humphreys and others – and said they had corrupt dealings with detectives. A detective chief superintendent was given the task of investigating these claims. The porn merchants denied having anything to do with sex mags (Humphreys refused to be interviewed); the Obscene Publications Squad detectives denied knowing the alleged pornographers or anything about them dealing in the trade. The chief superintendent took all this at face value and submitted his report, which was accepted by his superior. A few years later, Phillips, Citron, Mason and Humphreys would be convicted and be witnesses in the trials of bent detectives. Once again, the clear implication is that a Met "investigator" swept press allegations of police corruption under the carpet with a shoddy inquiry.

Nevertheless, having interviewed various pornographers, including Humphreys, read his diaries and gathered other evidence, Kelland was building a picture of police corruption in Soho. He asked for permission to expand his investigation beyond Rusty's complaint and received more staff and a Scotland Yard office on the same floor as the newly formed A10. At the same time, Robert Mark followed through on his instinct that enforcing the Obscene Publications Act on the streets of Soho should be given to uniformed officers. This broke the cosy, longstanding relationship between detectives and porn men, replacing it with policing by the uniformed branch, which would not be able to investigate any allegations of corruption in its own ranks.

In addition, the new Assistant Commissioner (Crime), Colin Woods, directed the Serious Crime Squad under Detective Chief Superintendent Bert Wickstead to launch an inquiry into the porn syndicates. Wickstead's integrity was not in doubt – Robert Mark wrote that Wickstead had "a bullet through his window one night", an indication of the threat he presented to villains. Feeling the heat, "King of Soho" Bernie Silver left the country.

Statistics also showed that the Obscene Publications Squad was not only corrupt but had not been doing its job. In the whole Metropolitan Police area, the amount of porn seized and the number of people prosecuted rose between 1968 and 1972, along with the number of searches conducted. Soho, however, bucked this trend – the number of shops searched in 1971 was half that of 1969: 63, down from 128.

Mark's new regime, however, was a long way from the complacency and sabotage that crippled investigations into *The Times'* allegations just three years before.

Kelland's dynamic investigation powered towards its endgame. Humphreys was caught in Holland, extradited and stood trial at the Old Bailey in 1974. After being sentenced to eight years for causing grievous bodily harm to Peter Garfath, he agreed to talk to Kelland and his team. Over three years there were more than 50 meetings between the investigators and Humphreys. As Humphreys gave more leads on the activities of bent cops and porn dealers, Kelland's team grew.

As the lines of inquiry developed, the detectives became interested in the swanky red Lancia that Bill Moody had driven, and which had aroused Frank Williamson's suspicions. Moody, now deprived of his Obscene Publications Squad power base, was stationed at Hammersmith, though in March 1974 he was on sick leave following a fall. Kelland's team discovered that the Lancia's previous owner had been George Vinn, a convicted pornographer. Vinn's story was that he sold the car to Moody.

Two of Kelland's detectives decided to interview Vinn's wife, Patricia, making sure George was not at home before they called. Patricia happened to deeply dislike Moody, whom she knew quite well having met him on various occasions with her husband. She gave the detectives the damaging news that her husband had given the Lancia to Moody in 1969 in return for helping George to avoid prison. At the time, Vinn had been charged with possessing obscene films at a Soho shop owned by John Mason. Mason, one of Soho's main players in the porn trade, was also grateful for the strings pulled by Moody, and gave the chief superintendent £14,000 (around £164,000 today) for the favour. Kelland brought Moody – complete with neck brace – in for questioning. Moody, unaware of Mrs Vinn's account, lied about his association with Mason and how he came by the Lancia. The case against one of the most powerful corruption brokers in Soho was building.

Where security had been a mess for Williamson's corruption investigation and vital documents had gone missing, Kelland's operation was tighter. It was a small team and all paperwork was locked away by a sergeant. However, Kelland was rattled when he heard from an informer that private investigators had been asking questions about him in London's West End. Because he had served for 10 years there, it was apparent that someone was digging around for compromising material that could be used to blackmail or compromise him. It looked like a sign that his investigation was a serious challenge to the corruption network, and it made him extra vigilant as he continued.

Once Humphreys started talking, the case against former commander Ken Drury became stronger. Humphreys, still bitter to have been declared by Drury to be a police informer, would testify against the ex-detective at his trial.

All the hard work of Kelland and his team paid off in February 1976 when 12 detectives were arrested, including the three senior men, commanders Wally Virgo and Ken Drury, along with DCS Moody. The charges were conspiring to receive money and "other considerations corruptly from persons trading in pornography". As Kelland would later write, "Such a scandal involving so many senior detectives – two ex-commanders, one ex-detective chief superintendent, one ex-detective chief inspector, four detective inspectors, two ex-detective inspectors and two ex-detective constables – had not occurred since the notorious Trial of the Detectives case in 1877."

The arrest of Drury, who lived in Sidcup, was described to this author by Don Williams, then a chief superintendent and Kelland's number two. "My sergeant and I went to get Ken Drury," he said. "When we arrived there, seven o'clock in the morning, there were lots of cars because the media were there. I went in to see the brains of Britain, Ken Drury. I said, 'Look, I'm awfully sorry about this, but there are people outside.' He said, 'I couldn't give a fuck.'

"So I asked him a few questions. We'd had information that Jimmy Humphreys had given him a rowing machine because he was a bit concerned about his weight as he was eating good food all the time. 'Yeah, yeah, I got that, it's over there.' And then I said something else about a watch somebody gave his wife. 'Oh yeah, got the watch.' That's corroboration, all these little things are corroboration [of his relationship with Humphreys]."

So Drury did not realise he was implicating himself by effectively acknowledging these "gifts" from the pornographer?

"No, he was that stupid. He was a commander of the Flying Squad and he was that bloody stupid. God, he was stupid. So I said, 'Right, come with us, let's go in the car.' And he ran and hid behind my car, so I took my coat off and put it over his head. And he sat in the back of the car like that. I took him in, and they [the arrested detectives] were all coming in [to Cannon Row police station]."

The arrests of the senior detectives were a shock and inevitably created headline news. Inside the Met, there was a mix of disbelief that so many were involved, combined with scepticism that the word of crooks could be trusted to implicate fellow officers.

Kelland's team, however, had worked diligently for three years to corroborate testimony, and the evidence would be tested at three big trials.

The first of what would be the three most serious corruption trials in the Met's history began in Number One Court at the Old Bailey on 8 November 1976. Two detective inspectors, a detective sergeant and three officers who had left the force were charged with conspiracy to accept money and other considerations from porn traders. Five were found guilty, and one inspector not guilty but was ordered to pay £2,000 in costs. He resigned before disciplinary proceedings began. Prosecuting counsel John Mathew spoke in court of "a cancerous growth of corruption" going back to the 1950s.

Trial number two began in March 1977. Virgo, Moody and four other men appeared on corruption charges. The court heard how Moody, on becoming an inspector in Soho in 1965, promised to organise the collection of bribe money better than ever. Young officers who did not want to join the corruption ring were ridiculed by Moody and moved on, or required to pay him a £100 fee to be transferred to another department. Virgo provided cover for Moody at commander level, as he did in the sidelining of Fred Lambert during *The Times* investigation. During the trial, the money being skimmed off the porn trade by bent cops was estimated at £100,000 a year (approximately £900,000 in 2022).

Virgo and Moody were convicted and received 12-year sentences (though Virgo's conviction was quashed the following year on the grounds that the judge had misdirected the jury). The other four men got sentences ranging between three and 10 years.

The final trial was that of Drury, Detective Inspector John Legge and ex-detective inspector Alex Ingram. It started on 14 June 1977. Legge was acquitted, but James Humphreys gave evidence of his corrupt dealings with the other two. Prosecutors said Drury received £5,000 (about £44,000 today) from Humphreys in weekly handouts of £100. Drury was sentenced to eight years, while Ingram, who had been corruptly dealing with Humphreys since 1964, got four.

The contrast between the Met's investigation into *The Times*' story – when Moody's machinations had amounted to a cover-up of the full extent of the corruption – and the Porn Squad inquiry was huge. With new Commissioner Robert Mark's backing, Kelland had the tools to rigorously investigate what had gone on for years. The convictions shocked many inside and outside of the Met, and the job had been challenging for Kelland personally. But as he said, "The crow of corruption had to be publicly nailed to the barn door."

Mark said Kelland deserved an honoured place in Met history: "But for the innocent who suffer in the meantime, in this case the majority of the Metropolitan force, it is easy to see the temptation to conceal, rather than expose, police wrongdoing in the supposed interest of the reputation of the force. It takes strong nerves and good judgement to see the need to put principle and probity first."

Kelland had the strong nerves and good judgement.

As the porn trials came to an end, Mark, Kelland, Williamson and everyone involved with A10 and anti-corruption could take a breather and feel some satisfaction at having completed an exacting and tricky job. The culture of rampant greed and cover-ups had been confronted and some of its major players jailed.

Corruption has evolved since the 1960s and 1970s into a new world of technology and crime syndicates that operate across borders today. *Line of Duty* reflects this. It portrays criminal involvement as police computer data is manipulated or leaked, bent cops collude with drug dealers and sex traffickers on council estates, while police manpower is stretched as never before.

In doing so, *Line of Duty* delves into the serious questions of fighting today's entrenched networks of corruption. Who is taking bribes? Who will testify against corrupt colleagues? Who can you trust?

Line of Duty revels in its convoy ambushes, shoot-outs and cliffhangers, but it deals with corruption seriously. Where Kelland suspected someone could be seeking a way to blackmail him, *Line of Duty* has PC Maneet Bindra and Sgt Jane Cafferty compromised and controlled by the Organised Crime Group. Bill Moody's diligence in sabotaging the probe into crooked detectives brings to mind Dot Cottan's endeavours to cripple

AC-12. Fred Lambert's brutal removal from the corruption investigation and disposal into early retirement is a harbinger of Ted Hastings' fate at the end of Series 6 – dumped from AC-12 and kicked into civvie street.

A day at the office is far more action-packed for Hastings than it ever was for Robert Mark, but the hit series works on two levels: it is undeniably thrilling entertainment but also thought-provoking.

It delves into how people are tempted to turn bad, how corruption works, and what kind of sacrifices are made to fight it.

5 - Fighting corruption – the making of Robert Mark

'There's only one thing I'm interested
in and that is catching bent coppers'

Confident, wily, confrontational. How did Robert Mark become
the man he was?

His roots were solidly working class. He was born in 1917,
the youngest of five, in the Manchester suburb of Chorlton-
cum-Hardy. While his father, John, had a limited education, he
rose from working in the manufacture of clothing to run his
own garment company of some hundred employees.

As his father's prospects improved, the family moved to a five-
storey house and young Mark got a place at grammar school.
However, the late 1920s was a period of recession and money
was always tight, the children walking one and a half miles to
school rather than paying the tram fare. Mark was a poor student,
distinguishing himself instead at rugby, cricket and lacrosse. In a
sign of things to come, perhaps, he also became head prefect.

On leaving school in 1935, he became a clerk/salesman for
a carpet firm. Prospects here were dismal and good jobs scarce
during the Great Depression, but after a couple of years, Mark
realised he had to find a new path. He was smart, fit and good
at physical pursuits, and decided that Manchester Police would
fit his attributes best. His father was horrified, suggesting that

becoming a copper was only one step better than going to prison. It would only be many years later, when Mark was Chief Constable of Leicester, that the older man acknowledged that joining the police had been a shrewd decision by his son. He began a thirteen-week police training course in 1937, and would later say of this moment, "Looking back, this was the end of Disneyland for me and the discovery of a world of harsh reality."

Real-world policing included juniors being bullied by senior officers and encountering his first dead body. New recruits were thrown in the deep end with four months of night duty. It was on his first day shift that Mark saw the body of a young man who had been crushed by a heavy lorry while riding a bike. A grim and terrible scene, but because Mark had not gone to pieces when dealing with it, his inspector assigned him to process all sudden deaths for the next few weeks.

The future straight-as-a-die Met Commissioner would later reveal in his autobiography that rules were sometimes bent or ignored. One dodge that beat officers practised occurred when they discovered suicides in a lock on the city-county border. If no members of the public had spotted the body, the bobby would press two shillings into the hand of the lock keeper. With this little bribe – or "perk" as Mark described it – the lock keeper would open the lock and flush the body through to the county side, thereby making it another force's problem to process. Mark admitted to doing this once, though on that occasion he suffered the indignity of finding the dead person back on his side the following day (seems the lock keeper was open to perks from both forces).

Another rule broken was carrying customised truncheons, which Mark did after an early selection for plainclothes work. "Most of us carried, wholly improperly, short rubber truncheons made in a nearby Dunlop factory," he would later write. This he used on one occasion when several officers were attempting to subdue an "enormous navvy", resulting in a broken shin for the struggling man. In plaster, the man appeared in court the next morning, paid his ten shilling fine, and went for a drink with Mark afterwards – there were no "hard feelings". Mark admits that in later years this incident would have resulted in a complaint, an inquiry, papers to the Director of Public Prosecutions, ending with a prosecution or discipline case. "Not that I didn't deserve it, but times were different, thank goodness," he recalled. The scourge of 1970s police wrongdoing had one or two blemishes on his own record.

Special Branch was Mark's next stop. At the time, this rather unglamorous role involved monitoring political factions potentially intent on breaking the law. With war looming, foreign groups or individuals were also of interest. An incident from this time roused in Mark strong feelings of regret and anger at the harm unthinking police work could cause. After Italy entered the war in 1940, Italian citizens resident in the UK were rounded up for internment or deportation. Mark was detailed to serve an order to a waiter called Ernani Landucci, who had worked in a Manchester hotel for some 30 years. Landucci burst into tears with the arrival of Special Branch. Mark said the order had to be served, but he told Landucci that he would report to his superiors that he felt the Italian, who had a British daughter, posed no threat. Three days later Landucci was dead. He had been placed by the authorities on a ship to Italy that was sunk by a German U-boat. The affair provoked the "strongest feelings in me", Mark said. It showed that "there was neglect, carelessness and worse in the police system. It was a lesson I never forgot."

During the war, Mark married his long-term partner, Kathleen Mary Leahy. They rented a semi-detached house, where they spent their honeymoon to a chorus of heavy anti-aircraft guns nearby. In 1942, with Britain in the middle of a desperate fight for survival against the Nazis, the government decided to release a portion of police officers for military service. Mark joined the armoured corps, applied for a commission and was trained at Sandhurst, where he became "fit, immaculately clean and turned into a near robot". He enjoyed Sandhurst, despite nearly drowning during training, and admired the instructors. He ended up with Phantom (GHQ Liaison Regiment) and would go on to lead communication patrols in Normandy and Germany. He witnessed some of the war's atrocities, such as murdered prisoners and cowering concentration camp survivors. His final wartime role was as a staff captain in the military government of Germany after the Nazis' defeat.

One legacy of his time in the army would be his ongoing belief in the efficiency and integrity of the uniformed ranks. In his time with the Metropolitan Police, he would often reveal his preference for the uniformed branches over plainclothes and for the deployment of well-drilled units such as the Special Patrol Group.

He returned home with a demobilisation suit, £5 and the honorary rank of major. He went back to policing in Manchester as a detective sergeant in Special Branch. Occasionally, he was loaned to CID, and found there that some interrogation practices made "my hair stand on end".

He described one senior detective he encountered in 1940s Manchester, when policing was "still a rough and tough business", who interpreted the Judges' Rules for treatment of suspects in his own way.

"Will you talk or be tanned?" was how this detective greeted prisoners. The uncooperative had their head shoved down the nearest toilet. Solicitors, counsel, judges and journalists all knew this went on, Mark said, and to pretend that it was a police secret was "sheer hypocrisy". This conspiracy of acquiescence existed because such practices were the only way to strike a balance between "the public interest and the rights of wrongdoers", he said.

Nevertheless, by the 1970s he was pleased to note that such violence was "strongly disapproved of by most policemen".

A constant theme in *Line of Duty* storylines is that cop work is full of grey areas when it comes to decision making. This ranges from Arnott and Fleming lying in Season 1 that Tony Gates died in the line of duty so that his family can get his pension (he actually commits suicide), to Hastings unofficially going undercover to infiltrate the OCG (Series 5).

Mark is forthcoming about unjustifiable police practices that went on around him during his early career. Another shocking incident from his autobiography is his account of an "old lag" called Taylor who, with three accomplices, severely assaulted an off-duty sergeant during a store break-in. Manchester officers scoured the neighbourhood for Taylor, found him and administered "first aid", a euphemism for a thorough beating. Taylor was then propped up unconscious before the magistrate. No one present, not policemen, detectives, journalists, solicitors, counsel, raised a protest about the condition of the accused man. Despite the "rough and tough" nature of early 1950s policing, Mark is clear that such retribution was disgraceful.

Further promotions came – inspector to chief inspector, superintendent to chief superintendent – and with them the extension of his experience from detective work to administration. Mark broadened his horizons further with a move to Leicester in 1957 as chief constable. He was 39 years old.

Policing in Leicester at this time was not the stuff of television crime dramas, however, and Mark's early preoccupation was dealing with the city's traffic problems. Leicester at this time was a low-crime area with a detection rate of 63 per cent. Cars, however, were causing chaos in the ancient city. Mark decided that the motorist, and the town council, had to be dealt with firmly. It was typical of him that he courted unpopularity to get this done. Henceforth, parking regulations were to be enforced to the letter, with no favour even for members of the county or city councils. Officers were sent out to enforce parking laws and ignore the status, wealth or politics of drivers as they did so.

The local papers, the *Mercury* and *Evening Mail*, were outraged by the new Chief Constable's regime (their delivery drivers now had to follow the rules). "Attila the Hun or Genghis Khan would have received kinder treatment at their hands than I did," Mark said. The parking battle showed Mark's tenacity in taking on vested interests and fronting up to opposition. He noted that his success reforming the flow of traffic and parking meant he was "loathed" by other chief constables, who faced similar problems and opposition. When dealing with Met corruption years later, he would show once again that for him, backing down was not an option when it came to enforcing the law.

It was while based in Leicester that Mark began to cultivate a public profile. His trenchant views on policing and the justice system found their way into lectures, public debates and book reviews. He came to be seen as a forward-thinking, articulate and reforming police chief. He had certainly been noticed in political and Home Office circles, so that when, at the age of 49 and after 10 happy years in Leicester, he found himself out of a job, he was not idle for long. The reason for his job loss was the amalgamation of his city's force with that of the county's.

Though Mark expected to retire from policing at this point, Home Secretary Roy Jenkins then invited him to lunch at the Hyde Park Hotel in London. Soon after, he was asked by the Home Office to represent the police on the Standing Advisory

Council on the Penal System, where he worked under Lord Mountbatten.

Perhaps it was Mark's forthrightness and outsider status that then prompted Jenkins to appoint him Assistant Commissioner of the Metropolitan Police. As we have seen, although the Commissioner, Sir Joseph Simpson, agreed to put up with Jenkins' choice, Simpson pointedly told Mark that the Met would not welcome him. Mark knew the Met had a tradition of producing its own senior officers at the Hendon Police College. He also knew his history: "I reflected that only one provincial policeman had ever been appointed to such high rank in the Met, Arthur Young, and he only lasted three years."

With some apprehension, Mark took up the London job in February 1967. He would later say of his arrival, "I had served in two provincial forces for 30 years, and though I had known wrongdoing, I had never experienced institutionalised wrongdoing, blindness, arrogance and prejudice on anything like the scale accepted as routine in the Met."

It reveals much about Mark that he was the interloper who had to keep his head down and grit his teeth before he found the right moment to step into the Met's top job. He was shown to his office, a "gloomy Victorian hovel" in the old Scotland Yard building, with a desk and rickety table.

Mark was Assistant Commissioner of D department, but no one took the trouble to explain to him what exactly he was supposed to be doing. Perhaps Commissioner Simpson and his deputy, John Waldron, hoped he would sit quietly and do nothing. Mark ate alone in his office – there was not even a mess for a lunchtime opportunity to mingle with colleagues.

When Simpson died in 1968, Home Secretary James Callaghan saw an opportunity to break the self-perpetuating hierarchy of the Met by imposing Mark on them. As we saw in chapter 2, Mark was shrewd enough to know it was not the right time for him.

Mark turned the job down, recommending that Deputy Commissioner John Waldron should be offered the position on a caretaker basis. He was due to retire in a couple of years, so the Home Secretary could use that time to better weigh up candidates to succeed him. Callaghan agreed, but placed Mark as Waldron's deputy, thereby giving him a chance to build his position in the Met.

Despite having such strong political support from the Home Secretary, it is clear that the Met establishment were effectively freezing Mark out and neutering him. Even when he became Deputy Commissioner with the prompting of Callaghan, Mark was given the full cold-shoulder treatment. "Thus began four of the most unpleasant years of my life, which might have ended more happily for those who sought my departure had they not provoked me so far as to arouse an overpowering determination to withstand all they could do," he would say later.

An inspiration for Ted Hastings

Mark and his fictional descendant Ted Hastings resemble each other most as outsiders, and being bloody-minded and determined to confront corrupt officers. Where Mark was a provincial cop imposed on the Met establishment, Hastings was doubly an outsider – first, as a Catholic officer in the largely Protestant RUC, and then as a former RUC man in AC-12. His past in Northern Ireland comes back to haunt him in Series 5 when he is suspected of having been responsible for the murder of DS John Corbett's mother, Anne-Marie McGillis, who was rumoured to be a police informer during the Troubles.

These formative experiences are what define them. Mark stealthily took on the old guard at Scotland Yard, while Hastings courted unpopularity as he faced bent coppers and opposition from his bosses.

Another similarity is that there are always lawyers provoking them. Mark spoke out against corrupt defence counsel; Hastings, of course, faces formidable foes in the shape of Organised Crime Group plant Gill Biggeloe, as well as the solicitor Jimmy Lakewell, another OCG stooge.

Mark and Hastings also share a rather outmoded attitude towards female colleagues. We see Hastings' hamfistedness in Series 4 when he has taken Steve Arnott to a bar and discusses his promotion prospects. Arnott is surprised when his boss says he would, of course, not be taking Kate Fleming to a bar for the same chat because she is an attractive young woman and it would not seem right. In the same series, Hastings is called out by DCI Roz Huntley for calling her "darling". His dealings with the opposite sex may be plodding, but by the next series it is clear that he does appreciate Fleming's accomplishments because it is she who has won promotion to the rank of detective inspector. Arnott, for the time being, remains a sergeant.

Mark reveals his own 1970s' brand of sexism in his autobiography. Here he says he gave way to "the blandishments of Henry Hunt, Assistant Commissioner", who had long wanted to introduce "girls into our corps". He was not talking about girls of school age, of course, but what we would today call women. He admits he was not easily persuaded. "They [women] are an expensive investment, because, on average, they serve under four years before leaving, usually on marriage." He also acknowledges his worries about having "120 nubile young women" at Hendon with 500 young men who were "full of go". His fears that Hendon would be turned into a scene from *Carry on Constable* proved unfounded. As Mark confirmed, they had 40 applicants for each job and were able to select top candidates.

For the sake of the drama, by the time we get to Series 5, Hastings is a seriously compromised figure. His marriage has fallen apart thanks to his misjudged financial investment. So abject does he become that he resorts to viewing internet porn in his grubby hotel room. (In contrast, Mark, who would receive a knighthood in 1973, was only ever a respectably married father of two.)

Where Mark tolerated a little rule-bending during his early days in policing, Hastings in contrast is put through the wringer when he goes rogue in Series 5 to infiltrate the OCG. This results in an accusation that he is "H", codename for a senior corrupt officer within his force, Central Police. As the character is pushed to his limits, he conducts an unrecorded, surreptitious interview in prison with OCG member Lee Banks. All this is to say nothing of the £50,000 Hastings had spirited away from the £100,000 "loan" he received from former detective Mark Moffatt and later anonymously gave to John Corbett's widow, Steph. So here Hastings was breaking all kinds of rules, even if his motives were noble.

It has to be said that these plot convolutions from Series 5 were at times tenuous and flaky. In a bid to make Hastings look suspicious, the character suddenly becomes somewhat stupid and reckless – accepting a suspect package from Moffatt, exposing himself to the OCG, stealing £50,000 – which did not do justice to the Hastings as developed in the first four series. One or two of these lapses might have been acceptable, but so many made Hastings appear a bit daft. At the end of the series, he is reprimanded with a finding of discreditable conduct over his unauthorised undercover shenanigans. Robert Mark would not be impressed.

Comparing where Mark and Hastings converge and differ is entertaining, but we come back to their shared outspoken integrity – rare in modern public figures – to explain why Mark is held up as a prototype for Hastings. When Dame Cressida Dick was forced out as Met Commissioner in February 2022, it was Robert Mark to whom she was compared. As a *Guardian* journalist wrote at the time, "Dick – appointed the first female commissioner in 2017 and, as our most prominent officer, the symbol for policing nationwide – never had the clarity of vision and purpose to follow Mark's well-documented example of how to effectively cleanse the rot from an organisation. Perhaps this is because to tackle such systemic problems, you have to admit they exist in the first place, something Dick singularly failed to do. Instead, as commissioner, she repeatedly employed the excuse that the horrific behaviour of Metropolitan police officers was the work of the odd 'bad 'un'."

To some extent, watching *Line of Duty* is wish fulfilment. We want to root for characters who say – as Hastings does – "There's only one thing I'm interested in and that is catching bent coppers." While Mark's version was, of course, that he wanted a CID that caught more criminals than it employed.

This brings us to another distinct reflection between fact and fiction – that of the way in which *Line of Duty*'s AC-12 (Anti-Corruption Unit 12) recalls the groundbreaking branch set up by Mark, A10.

On becoming Deputy Commissioner, Mark was able to tighten disciplinary procedures, with detectives returned to uniform and increasing numbers of them suspended. He also began to build alliances with other senior officers who were not members of the Hendon clan.

Mark's moment came when the Commissioner, Sir John Waldron, bemoaned the multiple scandals engulfing Scotland Yard – the "firm within a firm" allegations, the Porn Squad exposé, questions over the Drug Squad – and the increasing suspensions of his officers.

"What can the explanation be?" Waldron asked in frustration at a routine meeting. "It must be lack of supervision."

When Mark countered that the answer could actually be found in the totally unsatisfactory way in which the CID investigated criminal allegations against its own members, most of the senior officers present agreed with him.

"You're the de facto disciplinary authority," Waldron said. "Why don't you do something about it?"

Mark's adversary, Assistant Commissioner Peter Brodie, had left the UK on police business. As a result, Mark was able to use his absence to get the beleaguered Commissioner to allow him to set up A10, a squad separate from the CID that could independently investigate detectives under suspicion. Brodie instinctively believed in and usually protected his detectives, but A10 would smash the cosy arrangement whereby CID officers investigated their own. It would become the biggest challenge to entrenched detective corruption ever seen in the Met.

"Mark was clever," said Don Williams, who became an important member of Mark's A10 team. "Dead straight, knew what he wanted. I think he'd had a sickener of what he saw in the Met as a deputy. And in particular, the Williamson inquiry [into *The Times*' allegations of Met corruption]. That was an absolute sickener. And he was determined to do something about it. And the Commissioner of the day didn't have the balls to back him. So when Mark took over – bang! – A10 was founded."

6 – AC-12 – fictional descendant of A10

'No more beating around the bush'

Line of Duty's AC-12, like the real anti-corruption squad set up by Robert Mark in 1971 – A10 – was established to take down corrupt networks of officers. Sabotaged by bent coppers, resented and insulted, they needed dedication and fortitude to do a job that could exact a huge personal toll.

By the time a somewhat exasperated Met Commissioner Sir John Waldron asked Mark to do something about the breakdown in CID discipline, Scotland Yard was staggering from the effects of these multiple scandals.

Waldron's invitation to act was the green light for which Mark had long been waiting. He was affronted by CID officers in London virtually being a law unto themselves. Where allegations of corruption against officers in a provincial force would be investigated by an outside force, no outsiders were allowed to investigate the Met's officers. This had created a culture of near impunity for many seriously corrupt officers, in which investigations were sometimes "light" and law-breaking groups of officers escaped justice.

During his first three or four years in the Met, Mark gained first-hand experience of the force's self-serving attitude to discipline. For example, he was approached by two senior officers with a request to quash the suspension of a detective accused of corruption on the basis that he was a key witness in several criminal prosecutions. Those prosecutions might have been jeopardised if the detective under suspicion was under investigation himself.

Mark flatly refused to lift his suspension. That the two senior detectives felt able to approach the Deputy Commissioner with such a request shows that this was normal practice in Scotland Yard at the time. Mark wanted to boot the two out of the force, but the Commissioner would not back him in this. The accused detective was eventually dismissed from the force. Clearly, Mark was correct to think his suspension was fully justified. Of this incident, former A10 officer George Thomson-Smith told this author, "I hear that Mark was absolutely flabbergasted. I mean, he knew there was a sort of lax or even casual regard to complaints of wrongdoing. He knew that, but to get it in his own room…"

Though Mark had been ostracised during his first couple of years in Scotland Yard, he had gradually found one or two allies who shared his view that CID needed to be brought under control. As soon as the Commissioner gave him the go-ahead, Mark sat down with Jim Starritt, Assistant Commissioner, and two of his senior men, Henry Hunt and Ray Anning. Within 10 days they had come up with a blueprint for A10. This was taken for approval to Sir Philip Allen, Permanent Under-Secretary at the Home Office. They were determined to act quickly before Peter Brodie, Assistant Commissioner of C department, which had a monopoly on how its detectives were disciplined and investigated, could return from his trip abroad and neuter the plan.

Allen told Mark and his co-conspirators that the Home Secretary was delighted with the proposals.

A10 would be a jolting change from a century of CID self-governance. It would be a team of hand-picked officers, both uniformed and detectives, commanded by a senior uniformed officer under the Deputy Commissioner. The CID was no longer permitted to investigate crimes alleged to have been committed by its own officers. In addition, it would also inflict what was seen by many detectives as the indignity of having uniformed officers investigating the supposed elite of the detective branch.

With Mark having unveiled his A10 plan, and newspaper exposés of police malpractice continuing to be printed, the new Conservative Home Secretary, Reginald Maudling, summoned him. The Home Secretary said something along the lines of, "Are you going to do this ruddy job for us?" – meaning become Met Commissioner. Mark agreed on one condition: he wanted the power to move the assistant commissioners between departments. Maudling agreed. This suggests Mark would have shifted Brodie from his power base as head of the most powerful department, C. Brodie no doubt knew at this stage that he had lost the power struggle with Mark, the usurper from the provinces. Suffering from stress, Brodie left the service.

The Scotland Yard old guard had been hostile to Mark since his arrival in 1967, treating him with icy disdain. Now he, with the backing of the Home Office, was going to sweep them away and reform discipline. Having introduced A10, he then fronted up to CID and told them, as we saw in chapter 2, that they were the "most routinely corrupt organisation in London".

During his first month as Commissioner Designate, Mark had another face-off with the old guard. C department, which under Peter Brodie had been Mark's relentless adversary, sent round a file about its willingness to discuss the formation of A10 "with a view to saving the time of CID officers". Mark immediately met this early attempt to demarcate A10's work in his no-nonsense style. He circulated his written response to the senior officers of the Met: A10 was not about saving anyone's time. "It was a necessary innovation because no one had any confidence in the way C department investigated allegations of crime by its own members," he wrote in his autobiography. Most stinging, he made it plain that no one, no matter how senior, would be allowed to obstruct A10 in any way (a response Ted Hastings would no doubt wholeheartedly endorse).

Having played his cards close to his chest since his arrival at Scotland Yard as an unwanted and unpopular Assistant Commissioner – at least among Peter Brodie and his cohort of senior men – Mark, by 1972, felt confident that he could break the grip of the old guard. He had the backing of the Home Office, allies such as his deputy, Jim Starritt, uniformed officers and many in CID who were not involved in criminality.

In addition to setting up A10, he sought to break the power of the detectives by placing them under uniformed commanders. He switched policing of the pornography trade from the detectives to a uniformed commander, and he instituted regular interchange between uniformed and detective branches – all to prevent officers getting too cosy with the major criminals with whom they had to deal regularly.

CID's monopoly on dealing with hardened crooks and keeping their discipline in-house was shattered.

Joining the anti-corruption squad

Line of Duty depicts the struggles of Superintendent Ted Hastings, Detective Inspector Kate Fleming and Detective Sergeant Steve Arnott as they investigate ruthless corrupt officers.

When we first encounter Arnott in Series 1, he is in the stressful situation of being a whistleblower who refuses to help cover up the failures of a police raid that resulted in the death of an innocent man. He has several unprofessional sexual relationships during the following series (with a witness and a suspect) and becomes addicted to painkillers.

The pressures of undercover anti-corruption work also harm Fleming's relationship with the father of her son, who has custody of the boy. Meanwhile, Hastings is himself accused of being corrupt and makes some damaging professional decisions during the course of Series 5.

But what were the pressures like in the real anti-corruption squad A10?

Before becoming a leading member of the A10 team, Don Williams joined the Met in 1969, after serving as a police officer in Wales. On the Met's appointment board facing him were Robert Mark, Peter Brodie and Jim Starritt. Williams got the job and joined the uniformed branch as a chief inspector, later promoted to chief superintendent.

It was not long before he ran into trouble for breaching CID's exclusive status. After he signed a CID officer's work diary, Williams was sent for by the detective chief superintendent. He clearly felt Williams had interfered with the management of a Met detective, who was out of bounds to a uniformed senior officer in London. The plainclothes officer asked why Williams had signed the detective's diary. Williams recounted the exchange:

"'Because he's one of my men.'

"'No, he's not one of your men.'

"'Yes, he is.' I said, 'I'm the chief superintendent, he's one of my men.'

"'No, they're not. It's different from where you come from.'

"Basically, he was telling me I couldn't touch his man. I didn't like the sound of that, frankly."

This was the culture that Robert Mark challenged with A10 and his other reforms, putting uniformed officers in overall charge to break the stranglehold CID had on investigating itself.

"Bob Mark had become the Commissioner," Williams said. "He'd set up A10. It was a mixture of CID – usually junior CID – and uniformed officers just mixed together, classed as detectives."

Williams was open to becoming involved in anti-corruption because he had become aware of dishonest, venal practices among certain officers. "In the three years I was out and on divisions," he said, "I'd seen so much corruption in the Met."

In one incident he was part of a team setting up observation where an armed robbery was understood to be planned. It subsequently emerged that members of the Flying Squad were actually in league with the robbers for this crime. "So our people were at risk of getting shot for these bloody people."

Williams also cites the Luton post office robbery of 1969, in which sub-postmaster Reginald Stevens was shot dead, as one particularly bad case of police criminality. It would become clear later that once again Kenneth Drury, bent detective of Porn Squad infamy, was involved. He colluded with two suspects in the case to share reward money while incriminating three innocent men for the bungled raid. Patrick Murphy successfully appealed against his conviction in 1973; Michael McMahon and David Cooper were jailed until 1980, only having their names cleared in 2003, after both had died. One of Drury's officer colleagues and fellow Freemason would later say in a statement that Drury often took payoffs from crooks to help them avoid jail.

"They killed the postmaster," Williams said. "That's how bad things were. Instead of dealing with the murder properly, they were more concerned with... uh." Words failed him, but it was apparent he meant to say that rather than seeing the murderers brought to court, Drury was more concerned with getting a backhander.

Meanwhile, Williams had been noticed by Mark's team. He was asked by Jim Starritt, who became Deputy Commissioner, to look for proof that Flying Squad chief Ken Drury had been on a holiday with pornographer Jimmy Humphreys. Williams was the one who quietly and quickly found evidence of Drury's inappropriate trip, which enabled Robert Mark to make sure that the senior detective was immediately suspended.

As part of A10, Williams said, "We had Ray Anning as a commander in charge. He had been a uniform man all the way through, dealing with discipline, so he knew what was going on. And that was the start. And we had a couple of pretty good operations there.

"The best one I had was [to investigate] a detective inspector from the British Transport Police who was organising massive thefts [of goods in transit] from the Stratford depot, using the manager from the depot and his workers, paying them overtime to steal. We had got somebody on the inside of that with a tape recorder, and we got a massive amount of evidence.

"So, we went out and arrested about 20 people in one hit, bang, took them all into West Ham police station, had all the workers down in this big room."

He told the assembled arrested workers that he was not interested in charging them. He was after the detective inspector who was organising and paying them for the thefts. He wanted them to talk to him, then make a witness statement, and they would not be charged. "They thought about it and said, 'Yes, we'll do that.' So I had witness statements." The detective inspector was convicted.

Williams was subsequently summoned to see a commander called Tony Rounds. "And he said, 'You know Mr Kelland [Assistant Commissioner Gilbert Kelland]?'

"And I said, 'Yes, sir.'

"'So he said he wants you to volunteer to go and help him [investigate corruption].'

"I said, 'Do I have a choice, sir?'

"He said, 'Not really.'

"I said, "Well, I'll volunteer."'

Williams had been summoned to work on Kelland's A10-linked investigation into the Porn Squad. Despite being "volunteered", he had seen enough corruption in the Met to be eager to get involved.

It was Williams who helped to turn vital witness Tony Kilkerr, a detective inspector in Criminal Intelligence who would provide damning testimony in court against senior officers. One of Williams' sergeants told him that Kilkerr was unhappy. It turned out the inspector was a Scottish Presbyterian, excellent family man and fine detective. Williams was told that Kilkerr seemed troubled.

"So I had him in," Williams recalled. "We had a long chat, and I didn't push him or anything. But you get a feel sometimes, this guy wants to talk. And he said, 'I don't know what to do, to be honest, guv.'

"I said, 'What would you like to do? You know, it's in your hands. I can't force you.'

"He said, 'Can I go see my commander?'

"He came back to see me in the afternoon. 'Have you seen your commander?'

"'Yes, sir'

"'What did he say?'

"'He said, tell him [Williams] to get fucked.'

"I said, 'That's fair. What are you going to do?'

"He said, 'I'm going to tell you the story.'"

Williams told Kilkerr he did not want him to be seen coming to his office at A10. Even though the office was secure, he did not want anyone seeing and perhaps putting pressure on the inspector. So Williams arranged for Kilkerr to take a few days off to be interviewed at home. Kilkerr bravely revealed how, as a young detective sergeant with the Obscene Publications Squad, he was compromised by his boss. At the Friday night office drinks, the detective chief inspector pressed some banknotes into Kilkerr's hand, saying, "Here you are, here's your share." When Kilkerr refused the money, he was told not to be so bloody silly, it was the safest cash he would ever make. The money was pushed into his jacket pocket. Having had the money pressed on him, Kilkerr felt trapped.

However, after speaking to Williams and Kelland's team, he would give evidence against the detective chief inspector, George Fenwick, and four other former members of the Porn Squad. All were convicted at the Old Bailey.

A former detective superintendent, Michael Taylor, who is now in his 80s but had experience in A10 back in the day, made an interesting point about Kilkerr, whom he had known. He pointed out to this author that before A10, when a senior officer pressed a backhander into the pocket of a new officer, as happened with Kilkerr and others, there was no one the new recruit could turn to for help. And sometimes the corrupt payment might be for something serious, such as "buggering up", as Taylor put it, evidence in a prosecution case.

"A10 gave honest cops the chance to not fall for something that was illegal, corrupt, against the whole ethos of honest policing," Taylor said.

The A10 investigators also dealt with complaints against officers via a 24-hour hotline. "People could and did ring up any hour of the day or night complaining about policemen," Taylor said.

We see in *Line of Duty* Series 1 how Steve Arnott's refusal to go along with the cover-up of negligence in the police shooting of an innocent man marks him out as an officer of integrity for Ted Hastings to recruit. While recruitment was less dramatic in the real A10, good investigators were often headhunted for the work. Taylor revealed it was an innocent cup of tea in the canteen at Kentish Town police station during which he came to the attention of someone important.

Taylor was an inspector at the time, when the only other person in the canteen, a superintendent whom he had never seen before, asked him if he knew anything about a local villain. As a former sergeant at that nick, Taylor was able to give the senior man a great deal of background on the thief. "He obviously didn't expect a uniformed inspector to have a knowledge of the criminal fraternity in Kentish Town," Taylor said.

The make-up of A10 was designed to be a mix of uniformed officers and plainclothes detectives who would investigate CID without fear or prejudice. It was clear that on this day, the uniformed inspector Taylor had made an impression on the superintendent. A while later, after he had moved to a new role in West Hendon, Taylor said, "The chief superintendent came in and said, 'You've got friends. You're going to A10.' And that was it, I was hoicked out and off to A10. I had come to the notice of somebody I hadn't met before – the man who had the cup of tea in Kentish Town. It was by word of mouth and recommendation. Inquiries would no doubt be done when somebody's name was put forward."

While he knew anti-corruption work at Scotland Yard would be a challenge, and A10 officers were usually not popular with those in CID, it was a job Taylor knew was important. He had heard of money changing hands for a police officer to change his testimony to allow an accused thief to be acquitted. "Corruption certainly was a problem," he said. "Robert Mark set out, as he put it, to make virtue fashionable." Cases he became involved in included those of an alleged receiver of stolen goods, who told A10 an officer was demanding money from him, and a uniformed officer who took money through a publican to "square up" motorists' traffic offences.

Former detective superintendent John Simmonds described his mixed feelings on going to A10. "I got the call to go to A10," he said. "In one breath I was obviously pleased, but I was not happy that I was going to spend my time, day in, day out, investigating the bad side of the police service. There's no let-up, no fun side to it at all. It was sad that it was necessary."

Simmonds had no doubt about the effect A10 had on serving officers. Interviewed on the BBC documentary *Bent Coppers*, he said, "Fear of A10 was like the fear of the policeman walking the street. A10 became like the Bobbies on the beat for the police service."

Don Williams is scathing about officers at that time who turned a blind eye to wrongdoing. He said, "CID in the Met comprised of three groups of people: the corrupt, those who saw corruption and didn't have the balls to do anything about it, and those who were so incompetent they did not know it was going on. It [the Met] was a very corrupt organisation."

Having witnessed and heard of all this police corruption in his time in the capital, Williams had the motivation he needed to join A10 when asked. He would eventually be the man to arrest Ken Drury over the Porn Squad corruption, resulting in Drury's conviction in 1977.

It is sobering to reflect that had Mark not been on the scene at this point, keeping Drury in post would have seemed perfectly natural for the Scotland Yard powers that be. And you have to wonder whether the commander would have faced such a painstaking investigation and imprisonment under the old regime.

During his time with A10, Williams was stunned by the sheer level of corrupt money changing hands. One story the team picked up was that Commander Ken Drury and Commander

Wally Virgo had quarrelled over the share of money they were getting in kickbacks from the porn dealers in Soho. "The money from porn was massive," Williams recalls. "You wouldn't believe how much money." A meeting was called at a restaurant between the two senior officers and the two main players in the Soho porn world, Jimmy Humphreys and Bernie Silver.

At this meeting it was agreed that Humphreys and Silver would each pay them £2,000 a month not to interfere in the sale of illegal porn. "Now back in 1969, when this happened, I was on a thousand a year," Williams recalls. "Two thousand a month was big money. And every time they messed up the payment, they [Drury and Virgo] would be bunged 'a drink'. You know, a bung in those days was 50, 100 pounds. They were a couple of very wealthy men. That was one of the stories we were able to prove."

We saw in chapter 3 how detective "Wicked" Bill Moody, driver of flash cars and organiser of the Porn Squad corruption, had been an agent provocateur to derail the 1969 investigation into widespread police profiteering. Don Williams relates further extraordinary efforts of Moody's to protect criminals and his corrupt dealings with them – until A10 finally exposed him for the crook he was.

The first occasion involved a flooding in the basement of Holborn police station in Bloomsbury, London. The basement was where pornographic magazines confiscated from adult stores in Soho were kept, along with case files. The latter included a lot of cases in which the store staff had been charged with running an illegal operation. These staff arrested were not the genuine owners of the stores. They were fronts for the real owners and would give false names. If they appeared in court and were fined, they would pay up. If they were remanded on bail, they would disappear.

Following the basement flooding, all the porn and the case files were said to have been destroyed. This meant the accused "patsies" would never face trial and possible imprisonment, thereby protecting the real Soho kingpins who owned the shops.

"When this flooding took place in Holborn police station," Williams says, "it was a wonderful opportunity to get rid of all the files. Now we interviewed the firemen that went there…" The firemen revealed there was only a little water on the floor. "It wasn't flooding per se, but just water on the floor, and so the files could and should have been kept. But they destroyed the lot of them and got rid of a lot of cases.

"This was one of Wicked Bill's bloody little schemes to get rid of all these outstanding cases."

Moody's most audacious bit of skulduggery – so brazen even *Line of Duty* would probably not replicate it as a plot line – involved the setting up of a phoney court.

Cambridgeshire police had arrested some "toe rags" for something like housebreaking. It so happened these crooks were connections of Moody's that he wanted to protect from facing trial. "So they invented a fake court in Tintagel House and Wicked Bill Moody was the magistrate," Williams says.

The Cambridgeshire police were hoodwinked into believing their suspects were being dealt with in a genuine magistrates' court. "Magistrate" Moody turned down the police request to remand the men in custody and granted "bail". The men went free, and the provincial police, no doubt disappointed with the outcome, believed they had been dealt with in a real court.

Williams said he heard of this extraordinary deception from Frank Williamson and Detective Chief Superintendent Charles Naan, two of the team that were thwarted by Moody when they were investigating *The Times'* 1969 exposé of police corruption. While Williamson was Her Majesty's Inspector of Constabulary, Naan was one of his trusted provincial officers on the corruption inquiry.

"Williamson got in touch to have a chat with me and tell me one or two things that happened to him," Williams recalls. "He gave me a lot of background to what was going on. It made us realise the lengths these people would go to cover up.

"I know it sounds ridiculous, but that happened. It was appalling what was going on, really appalling."

Bill Moody was a one-man wrecking ball, hampering all efforts to uncover CID wrongdoing and protecting the lucrative level of corrupt payments from the porn trade. In the *Line of Duty* universe, it is DI Matthew "Dot" Cottan who is perhaps the embodiment of Moody, as he schemed across three series to thwart AC-12, frame Steve Arnott and protect the Organised Crime Group.

Back in the real world, bent detectives who knew they might be targeted by A10 often tried, much as their fictional counterparts in *Line of Duty* do, to sabotage Don Williams and his colleagues.

"You can imagine the kind of threats put on you," Williams said. "Phone calls to your wife telling them their husband's not doing the job, he's out having affairs and all that sort of stuff. There was a lot of that taking place.

"That's why we had to keep ourselves very closed. We had a couple of office suites that were bolted and barred. I had a very small team. On a Friday night, we'd come into my office, we'd have a couple of beers, fool about a bit just to get the pressure off, you know, just to relax and have a bit of fun. We did that every Friday night."

Another tactic was to suggest innocent targets for A10 to investigate, to give the team the runaround. Williams recalled, "One of these fellows said to me, 'You want to start investigating [Deputy Commissioner] Jim Starritt.' So I said, 'Okay, let's do that. Can you tell me exactly what I'm going to be investigating?'

Because it was just bullshit. They were just trying to throw curveballs at you to make you go off in the wrong direction."

The bent detectives were implacable foes. "These guys, they really would stop at nothing if they could get away with it," Williams said. "But in the early days of A10, we were fairly powerful because we had powerful people with us. By that I mean Gilbert Kelland and Jim Starritt.

"Speak to people in the CID at the time, they were really shit-scared of A10. A10 was straight. You know, they did the job."

Where it had been relatively straightforward for Bill Moody to sidetrack and sabotage the investigation into *The Times*' allegations, corrupt officers knew they could not take A10, or its successor, CIB2, lightly.

Jackie Malton, former Flying Squad detective, recalled, "They [anti-corruption officers] instilled fear in other police teams, whether they'd done something wrong or they hadn't. They would come in and do a sweep – they did one in my station. They'd just come in and do what you'd call a bin spin." CIB2 would turn up and go through all the files on everyone's desk, even if there was no evidence of corruption. "It was just something that they'd come in and do, a bin spin. Whenever you were called to their office, it always instilled fear. It did feel like they were the enemy.

"I'd been called up to CIB to help when people had made a complaint, and you've got to go through that process. Even though you haven't done anything wrong, you're checking your paperwork, the pocket book, you're checking that everything is correct. I think that what *Line of Duty* does get right is the fear that they can instil."

Speak to officers of this period, most of whom are in their 80s now, and they all make a similar point. A10's officers followed the rules and were "straight" in dealing with accused colleagues, even in the most difficult situations.

"It wasn't a place where you had a lot of laughs," Michael Taylor said. "Some of it was quite unpleasant." The second worst job police officers had, after informing relatives that a loved one had died, was to execute a search warrant at a police officer's house in the presence of his family. "That's not a pleasant thing to do," Taylor recalled. "But you do it properly. And I never saw any heavy-handed behaviour in there. You knew with most people the allegations were true and they were going to lose a job or were going to go to jail. And you just dealt with them absolutely correctly.

"The A10 I joined was run by its first commander, a man called Ray Anning, for whom everyone had a great deal of respect. Very pleasant, very straightforward, decent man. If a detective was doing something that was criminal, he had to face the consequences." A10 was not about entrapment, "putting temptation in people's way, then going, gotcha," Taylor said. "We dealt with stuff that came our way as straightforward complaints against police. And I think we had a reputation for doing things in a straightforward fashion."

George Thomson–Smith, who had been a detective chief inspector with the Complaints Investigation Bureau (2) in the early 1980s, said the work entailed careful intelligence gathering of the kind that would not make good television drama. "The idea of the then commander was to concentrate resources on some serious people and tap their phones, follow them around," he said. Car chases and confrontations were scarce.

Don Williams emphasised that A10 painstakingly built its cases. It took some three years to gather evidence and testimony, corroborating everything, in order to bring a case against the Porn Squad in 1977. Williams says there was never any "verballing" – the concocting of incriminating statements for suspects to sign – or underhand tactics against detectives they were investigating.

He even makes a rueful comparison to the popular interrogation scenes from *Line of Duty*.

"We didn't have tape recorders and all that sort of stuff," he said. "When you did an interview, you had to have it written down. So when we were ready to do the interview, we prepared a broad set of type-written questions. If he says this, we go to that question; if he says that, we'll go to this question. And then we'd write down his answer and sign it before we went on. So there was no question of being verballed or anything. These days, as you saw with *Line of Duty*, it's all recorded. Bloody marvellous."

The diligent work meant Williams never heard a complaint from an accused officer about their treatment by A10's investigators. And this was sometimes from bent detectives who had themselves used illegal tactics to convict criminals. Williams said some of those he caught and got convicted told him he had been "straight" with them. "So, now, that's praise from the people you put down," he said.

Today, police corruption is not as brazen and cavalier as it was in Mark's day. The head of the Flying Squad is not likely to jet off on holiday with a career criminal and their wives, and then claim he was hunting for a notorious bank robber while there. Having had so little scrutiny for the best part of a century, the bent detectives had grown complacent.

Line of Duty does a compelling job of capturing how shadowy and internecine the battle against corruption is in the 21st century. Superintendent Ted Hastings has confronted criminals embedded in his force, external gangsters, fellow Freemasons, corrupt superiors and his own professional rivals. Most of the action is, of course, played out in the AC-12 building, based in the fictional Kingsgate area of "the City".

Anti-Corruption Unit 12 is one of several professional standards departments in the fictional *Line of Duty* world, alongside AC-3 (dealing with the East Midlands force) and AC-9 (investigating corruption and running witness protection).

At the climax of Series 6, Hastings loses control of AC-12 to his icily efficient superior, Detective Chief Superintendent Patricia Carmichael. She and Chief Constable Philip Osborne proclaim to have little trust in Hastings and his team. AC-12 is to have its budget cut and be merged with AC-3 and AC-9.

Osborne is, of course, the officer who pressed Arnott to help cover up the shooting of an innocent man in a bungled police raid right back in Series 1. So as events are left hanging at the end of Series 6, it looks as though, despite AC-12's successes against the Organised Crime Group, it is Osborne – the epitome of turning a blind eye to wrongdoing to protect the force's reputation – who has won the day.

Robert Mark overcame the hostility of the Scotland Yard establishment to emerge as the Met's most renowned anti-corruption Commissioner. But for all his successes in changing the Scotland Yard culture, Mark had won a battle, not the war.

That is a pattern that repeats itself in *Line of Duty*. Hastings brings down the quartet of bent senior figures known as "H" – Biggeloe, Hilton, Cottan, Buckells – but it is clear that undetected forces of criminality still lurk in the corridors of Central Police.

In Robert Mark's 1970s period in charge, A10 was successful in rooting out hundreds of suspect detectives, but despite this, collusion with criminals still thrived in one part of the capital – the City of London.

7 – Colluding with criminals

'When did we stop caring about honesty and integrity'

In Series 5 rogue undercover cop John Corbett has infiltrated the Organised Crime Group and convinced them to launch a raid on the Eastfield police depot. At some point during this raid a mysterious corrupt senior officer will turn up. Not only is the senior officer sanctioning the robbery, but gang member Lisa McQueen has bribed security guards and drivers at the facility to stay out of the way. Gangsters and bent cops are allies.

This is a high-tension set piece in the series, as the gang – Corbett, Miroslav Minkowicz, Ryan Pilkington and others – take control of the depot and help themselves to a warehouse full of confiscated drugs, gold and cash. After the mystery officer – Detective Chief Superintendent Lester Hargreaves – is inadvertently shot to death by Corbett, the gang gets away with £50 million in valuables.

This kind of collusion between police and armed robbers has been drawn from real life. This bent partnership, in which robberies were committed and effectively sanctioned by certain bent detectives, is another major area of corruption that mired the capital during the 1970s.

New Commissioner Robert Mark was encouraged that he was making progress against corrupt networks in Scotland Yard. While A10 and his anti-corruption purge reduced the level of collusion between criminals and corrupt officers, robberies in particular declined while arrests were on the increase. In 1974 there were 98,000 arrests, up 11 per cent on the previous year.

Bank robberies plummeted from 65 in 1972 to 26 in 1973 and then 17 in 1974. A specially formed Robbery Squad – more intent on catching armed robbers than doing business with them – had great success against the hardened gangs.

"The Flying Squad, the Regional Crime Squad, the Robbery Squad and the Serious Crime Squad were all achieving successes on a scale never before experienced, largely because at long last they enjoyed the trust of CID, uniformed and provincial colleagues alike," Mark would later write.

However, the stink of corruption still permeated one area of the capital – the City of London, an area not overseen by Robert Mark and the Met. It was here during the mid-1970s that a Wild West of corrupt alliances between detectives and armed robbers played out, sometimes with lethal consequences.

During this period, suspects were being arrested for the many robberies being carried out in a small area. However, evidence seemed to get watered down or the accused were getting bail. Rumours went round suggesting dodgy deals were being done. City of London CID was being talked about. This was the era of the meticulously planned heist, which often resulted in big pay days for blaggers thanks to assistance from bent detectives.

On 3 May 1976 four men in wigs and boiler suits targeted the payroll of the *Daily Express* newspaper. Four days later a City of London constable came across a vehicle in which there were spent shotgun cartridges and empty bank money bags. When he informed the Control Room that he may have found the vehicle used in the *Express* robbery, he was told he was wrong, the actual vehicle had been chased in north London before being lost. The constable did not think any more of it, but it seems suspicious now that what might have been the robbery van with vital clues in it was purposely excluded from the investigation.

The City of London police were outside of A10's jurisdiction. Their beat was the square mile of the City, the banks, financial sector, Fleet Street. During the day, quantities of cash – payrolls and deposits – were being moved around. This tightly packed neighbourhood was a magnet for armed gangsters. There were 38 raids on Securicor vans in one year, of which 33 were successful.

One was attacked on 27 September 1977 outside Williams & Glyn's Bank on Birchin Lane. The van driver was shot in the leg and the six robbers snatched £500,000 in salary money. Later, six suspects were arrested, but all were freed on bail. As former Met commander John O'Connor said in a BBC documentary recently, "They went to court and bail wasn't objected to. It's up to the police to object to bail. These people are dangerous criminals, they pose a risk to the public, somebody had been shot. How do you get bail on something as serious as that? That is really ringing the alarm bells."

It would later become clear that money was being exchanged to water down evidence and get bail fixed.

Lew Tassell was a young detective constable, an exhibits officer whose job was to log evidence that had been found and by whom. Detective Chief Inspector Phil Cuthbert was his superior, the head of divisional CID, a confident, popular officer. One day around this time, outside the incident room, Cuthbert handed Tassell £50 in notes. "Lew," he said, "I've got a drink for you" – a drink meaning a bung or bribe. Tassell may have been surprised, but he did not say anything. As we saw with Tony Kilkerr in the previous chapter, this was how newbies were initiated into the ranks of the corrupt.

Cuthbert later gave the young detective another £50 "drink" money in front of other officers, which totalled £150 from his boss up to that point – around £1,000 in today's money. Tassell recalled in a 2021 BBC documentary: "There was no one I could go to and say, 'Look, I've been given this.' It would be ridiculous to even think that. Because he would have had to report it to someone, and it would have been investigated and nothing would have happened, except I would have been out of CID, that's for certain."

This is how young officers the world over are initiated into corruption. One thing Tassell was sure of: if he was getting £50, the more senior men were getting much bigger handouts. DCI Cuthbert would later go on trial for accepting bribes, with a man called Alf Sheppard saying he acted as middleman in negotiating bail or getting evidence fixed for armed robbers. Sheppard would later admit to BBC reporter Graeme McLagan that he handed out more than £80,000 as go-between for the robbers and Cuthbert. The chief inspector ended up being sentenced to three years for corruption in 1982. He was accused of doing deals with the Williams & Glyn's robbers as well as the men involved in the subsequent theft of the *Daily Mirror* payroll.

The City of London police had formed an armed unit to patrol the streets to deal with armed raiders. It was meant to be deployed as fast as possible, and it should have been patrolling on 31 May 1978, following a tip that a raid was going to be carried out. Suddenly, everyone was summoned to a scenes-of-crime lecture at Wood Street police station.

"First time ever we had a scenes-of-crime lecture," said Derek Smith, a former City of London inspector. "Very odd."

Commander Hugh Moore was to give the lecture. A constable came in and handed Moore a note. Smith said, "He looked up and smiled at one of his senior ranking officers and read out that there had been an armed robbery at the *Daily Mirror* building, the area that we were supposed to be patrolling. Our sergeant kicked a chair across the room at the Commander – he just laughed at us."

The implication was that the lecture had been arranged to clear the armed police patrol off the streets, so it was safe for the robbers to hit the *Mirror*. On this sunny May day, as guards unloaded cash from a Security Express van at the *Daily Mirror*'s former headquarters in Holborn, they were attacked by a gang of armed men.

Tony Castro, one of the guards, fought back. He was blasted at point-blank range and died as he was being rushed to hospital.

In 2021, looking back at the callous crime, the *Mirror* reported, "The vile attackers managed to escape with £200,000 and a sinister secret network of corrupt police officers made sure they never faced justice, which would provide inspiration for BBC drama *Line of Duty*."

In the end, eight men would be arrested in connection with the three armed robberies. All charges against them would eventually be dropped.

Lew Tassell would say later, "These suspects were, as far as we were concerned as junior police officers, responsible for the robberies. There's a guy murdered, he was killed by someone who shouldn't have had their freedom at that time. I thought, *This isn't why I joined the police.*

"I knew Phil Cuthbert was bent because he'd given me the money. I could assume 10 other people were bent because if he was going to give me money, he was going to give them money as well."

Cuthbert's conviction came after he was recorded revealing how the corruption process worked in the City of London. The man who caught him was the detective John Simmonds, who had served with A10 and became head of CID in the City in June 1978.

Simmonds was Cuthbert's boss. Both men were Freemasons, and Cuthbert, who feared he was going to be prosecuted, asked to speak to his new boss off the record, believing his brother Mason would not break the confidence. He then told Simmonds about corruption in the City of London force and how money from armed robbers had been paid to its officers. Simmonds told the BBC documentary *Bent Coppers* in 2021, "I withdrew my Freemason hat and put my police helmet back on... I realised that this was exceedingly serious."

Cuthbert assumed his new guv'nor and fellow Mason would back him "if he came unstuck". Simmonds knew he would need corroboration if he was going to challenge this deep-rooted corruption in his squad. In the shadowy world of police and criminals, it is notoriously difficult to ever get at the truth, certainly in a court of law. *The Times'* journalists had used an elaborate network of tape recorders to get their evidence of Met wrongdoing in 1969. Simmonds went for the same solution.

"I got fitted with a microphone," he said. "I was not proud that I was doing it, but I never lost sight of the fact that a man had got killed on one of the robberies. People were taking blood money."

The tape captured Cuthbert's revelation that the *Express* robbers paid detectives £20,000 to avoid prosecution, which would amount to more than £100,000 today. Cuthbert even alleged that the head of Scotland Yard's Robbery Squad and his team had taken money for helping three of the men arrested. He said he used to "bung" officers and "it used to go up to the fucking top of the tree, used to go up to the AC [Assistant Commissioner]".

He would also claim, "It's happened in the Met, it's happened in the City, it's happened in all the counties. It's happened for years and years."

Cuthbert's comments revealed that the firm within a firm still existed, while perhaps morphing into new forms.

Robert Mark had retired as Commissioner in 1977, partly in opposition to the 1976 Police Act, which proposed to transfer some responsibilities for discipline from chief officers to political appointees. He had been the country's top policeman for four years and 11 months and had succeeded in changing the culture of CID immunity from serious scrutiny. Setting up A10 and rebalancing authority between uniformed and detective branches had created a shift in mentality at Scotland Yard, and in how the public perceived allegations of corruption were being tackled.

However, corruption had obviously not been wiped out.

Far from it.

Old habits die hard at the Met

This became the age of the supergrass, criminals who informed on accomplices or associates in return for reduced sentences. From such sources, stories began to be heard of deals between the City robbers and local detectives. The government was alerted and Operation Countryman set up in 1978.

The name of the operation, to be run by Dorset police, was thought to be a disdainful dig by Met officers at the provincial officers. It was originally intended to be a probe into the City of London force, but their remit was extended to the Met, who referred to the outsiders as "the Sweedey". This was an insulting comparison, of course, with the dashing, brasher kind of Flying Squad policing depicted in the hit TV series *The Sweeney*, starring John Thaw. If nothing else, at least Robert Mark's mantra that the Met's CID should not investigate allegations against its own officers was being followed. Arthur Hambleton, Chief Constable of Dorset, was to head Countryman, with his assistant, Leonard Burt, as operational head.

The Met offered Countryman's dozen detectives a Portakabin in the yard of a south London police station as accommodation. Burt turned to Frank Williamson for advice. Williamson was the man who had had rings run round him by DCS Bill Moody when he had investigated *The Times'* 1969 allegations of deep corruption in the Met. Williamson's first piece of advice to Burt had been to have a secure office, because he knew all about important documents and action books going missing. So the Portakabin would not do. Countryman got off to a bad start when Burt asked for an upgrade and got no reply from the Met. Countryman's HQ was moved to secure premises in Godalming, Surrey.

Countryman has gone down in history as an acrimonious failure, but its one success was the tapes John Simmonds sent to Burt of Cuthbert's indiscretions about City of London and Met corruption. "One of the sergeants only got £300," Cuthbert is heard to say to Simmonds in a pub. "That was his share out of the 20 grand, and he got the fucking hump with it, thought it was a liberty… a lot of money changed hands, guv'nor."

Despite Cuthbert saying that Met officers, in addition to those in the City of London, had got a "drink" out of assisting the bank robbers, Burt had a hard time trying to effectively expand his probe into Scotland Yard. He pulled in 100 officers from provincial forces, rejecting any who had previously served with the Met. He also tried to make sure their investigations were untainted by slack policing – no socialising with Met officers, no free drinks, even a coffee, no free phone calls (this was before mobile phones).

There were also strict rules for obtaining testimony from criminals. No promises of immunity (that was to be decided by the Director of Public Prosecutions), any lying in a statement would result in a prosecution of wasting police time.

The Met was seriously irked by all of this. Had not Sir Robert Mark cleaned up Scotland Yard? The view of some was that Countryman was out of order going into prisons to drum up corruption allegations from criminals with nothing to lose.

While the Countryman team had compiled a hit list of 100 officers to check out – the vast majority being Met officers facing allegations of perjury, corruption, conspiracy – they also began to encounter roadblocks. Requested files would vanish or take weeks to turn up, and Burt's officers suspected the Met's hierarchy of tipping off detectives that they were planning to question. They could not tap the phones of officers under suspicion because the UK's interception system was owned by the Met.

There were structural problems with the Countryman set-up too. Dorset was a small force and its investigators were overwhelmed with corruption allegations. What was true? What was rubbish? What should they devote precious time to? Information overload became a challenge.

By 1980 the Met's counter-offensive was full-blooded. Countryman was out of control was the charge, having spiralled from a probe into three City robberies to take on the whole of the Met. Arthur Hambleton hit back: "Basically, you may say that we were stopped from cleaning up the Yard."

Simmonds' take on the investigation was this: "Once it started to get up into the ranks, I believe the Metropolitan Police wanted to whitewash this in order to ensure the public were not exposed to serious evidence of corruption by senior police officers."

Countryman ground to a halt with a whimper. Having taken 2,000 statements, pursued 200 corruption allegations and submitted 41 reports to the Director of Public Prosecutions, only four cases went forward. Of these, just one trial resulted in convictions. In addition to Phil Cuthbert being sentenced to three years, his assistant, former detective sergeant John Golbourn, got two years.

Scotland Yard was delighted in 1982 to have finally seen off Countryman. Met Deputy Commissioner Pat Kavanagh said, "Countryman has done great harm to our reputation. I will not have another one… Countryman is an argument against independent investigations rather than an argument for." He claimed the days of a "firm within a firm" were history and any corruption still around was perpetrated by lone officers, the inevitable reference to rotten apples. The Yard needed no help in dealing with them.

This all felt a little reminiscent of how the investigation into *The Times'* corruption allegations failed to look beyond the two detectives who were convicted, even though one of them, DS John Symonds, had originally stated that they were part of a wider "firm within a firm". Such complacency carried on into the 1990s, quietly burying the vigour of the Mark years.

Fighting the police establishment in *Line of Duty*

So, within a few years of Mark stepping down as Commissioner, the Met showed it had not lost its ability to close ranks against outside scrutiny. It may just about have swallowed the imposition of A10, but it could still derail the best the provinces had to offer. There are now, and were back then, detectives who felt the Countryman team really were bumpkins who lacked the expertise to build a case against Met detectives facing allegations.

However, it is hard not to suspect such opposition was the institutional reflex to first and foremost protect the Met's reputation, an instinct reinforced by decades of playing down the full extent of any wrongdoing. As a disillusioned Leonard Burt said after Countryman fizzled out, "People get what they deserve. If they're not prepared to put in the effort to sort something out, then they deserve what they get."

The implication being that the Met had not been willing to sort out the corruption that had helped to facilitate the City of London robbery spree.

Hostility to provincial officers, like that towards the uniformed branch, was not shared by Robert Mark. His own background was in the provinces, in Manchester and Leicester, and he had been disgusted by the criminality he found when he arrived at Scotland Yard. Despite his enforcing greater discipline and establishing A10, the old resistance to scrutiny and knee-jerk protection of the Met's image did not go away when his term finished.

Since then, the job of Met Commissioner has overwhelmed several high-flying officers – most recently, Dame Cressida Dick – while combating ingrained corruption has perhaps become more difficult than ever.

Line of Duty has dramatised the fierce challenge of modern anti-corruption work with insight drawn from the real-life crises in policing. Its depiction of Superintendent Ted Hastings' attempts to run exemplary investigations while dealing with bent officers and self-serving superiors has been gripping and often thought-provoking.

Philip Osborne is a character who epitomises the way reactionary forces can keep reasserting themselves at the top of law enforcement. His meteoric rise from chief inspector to chief constable bookends the six series. He goes from attempting to bully Steve Arnott into a cover-up in Series 1, when they are both in Counter Terrorism, to suspiciously emerging as top cop in Series 6. In episode 2 of that series, Hastings says it is an "outrage" that the commanding officer of the disastrous operation in which innocent man Karim Ali was shot by armed officers should now be "made chief".

In episode 4 DCC Andrea Wise reveals that Osborne is going to restructure Professional Standards, merging Superintendent Hastings' AC-12 with sister bodies AC-3 and AC-9. This will be headed by an officer senior to Hastings and have its budget slashed by 90 per cent. Hastings is, of course, infuriated, calling Osborne a "bare-faced liar" who is in thrall to politics and the Organised Crime Group.

Should *Line of Duty* return for its rumoured and much-anticipated seventh series, it is nicely poised for a brutal clash of cultures between Hastings-Arnott-Fleming and the new regime of Osborne. The new chief has already declared war, slamming over-zealous Professional Standards officers such as Hastings and his AC-12 colleagues, who he claims are undermining good honest coppers on the streets and harming public trust.

The parallels with real events here are irresistible, ranging from claims in 1972 that suspending Commander Ken Drury for holidaying with a crook would damage the morale of fellow officers to Deputy Commissioner Pat Kavanagh's assertion that the Met did not need independent scrutiny. In 2021 there were raised eyebrows as Commissioner Cressida Dick played down wrongdoing as the act of the occasional "bad 'un" in the Met, despite a blizzard of scandals engulfing the force.

By the end of Series 6, Osborne has got his way and started fast-tracking his "reforms". Detective Chief Superintendent Patricia Carmichael, Hastings' formidable antagonist, has been put in charge as new head of the shrunken, merged anti-corruption force. Hastings is bundled into retirement after 30 years' service. If the Organised Crime Group hoped to weaken the threat Hastings' team presented to them, they could have done worse than Osborne's reforms.

Will Osborne turn out to be simply an ambitious, self-serving, complacent chief constable in a seventh series? Or is he, as seems increasingly likely, a puppet of the OCG?

The actor who plays him, Owen Teale, said after Series 6 was broadcast, "I'm now defending myself in the shops, with people saying, 'I know you're "H".' And I go, 'No, no, no, no, wait a minute, we all know who "H" is now,' and they go, 'No, I don't believe that for a second. There's no way he would have had the power to do that. But your character was the original.'"

It is tempting to see in Osborne something of Robert Mark's arch-enemy at Scotland Yard, Peter Brodie. The consensus of those with experience of Brodie in the 1970s was that while he was not bent himself, he effectively covered up for criminal detectives by being blindly loyal to CID and denying there was any corruption. If anything, however, Osborne looks more dangerously proactive in disrupting anti-corruption efforts.

Brodie followed the advice of scheming Commander Wally Virgo to remove the honest Detective Chief Superintendent Fred Lambert from *The Times* inquiry. This cleared the way for DCS Moody to replace him. Moody, who was Virgo's partner in Soho corruption, then did everything he could to sabotage the investigation into *The Times*' allegations. This included paying £2,000 to one of the bent detectives under investigation, John Symonds, to flee abroad so he could not give evidence or expose the true number of grafting detectives.

The suspicion with *Line of Duty*'s Osborne must be that he will be more Moody than Brodie. In episode 5 of Series 6 we learned he had links to corrupt DCI Marcus Thurwell (a fleeting appearance by James Nesbitt in a photograph) and the cover-up around the death of Lawrence Christopher (a character loosely reflecting the real-life racist killings of Stephen Lawrence and

Christopher Alder). The Hastings-Osborne-Carmichael ménage should make for quite a tussle in any forthcoming storylines. Hastings would again need all of his skills in surviving the machinations of criminals masquerading as colleagues.

The City of London robbery scandals, the Countryman probe, with accompanying Scotland Yard resistance, give an insight into how cut-throat real police infighting can be among senior officers. Some officers made huge sacrifices to root out corruption, while unscrupulous officers subverted justice to enrich themselves, and a few senior figures appeared more concerned with protecting the reputation of the force at all costs.

In the fallout, criminals escaped justice, and some bent officers retired to enjoy the pension pots of corrupt money they had put aside. The careers of quite a few decent officers suffered, either through the frustration of failing to build cases against detectives who were effectively criminals, or through a heavy personal toll.

Line of Duty is imbued with the cynical and ruthless nature of this world. It also does justice to the grim price many anti-corruption officers pay in personal terms. Hastings, Fleming and Arnott have all been put through the mincer in their war with the OCG. Seeing the toll paid by the characters – and their real-world counterparts – it is hard not to feel moved and shocked.

8 – The high price of confronting bent colleagues

'We've been round the houses, Steve. Round
the houses and down the bloody drains'

Line of Duty does not hold back in depicting the personal toll
anti-corruption work takes on Ted, Kate and Steve. But the
stigma attached to their job is less than it was in the 1970s, when
the real A10 was set up to fight wrongdoing in the Met. While
anti-corruption investigation is today accepted as legitimate and
necessary work for men and women to apply for, confronting
seriously corrupt officers has always come with heavy personal
pressures and risks.

The high stakes are portrayed from the first episodes of *Line
of Duty*. DCI Tony Gates, the detective under investigation, is
disdainful of his pursuers. Colleagues shun Hastings and Steve
in the pub. DC Nigel Morton spits in Kate's hair when she is
exposed as an undercover AC-12 officer. Steve, who is known
to be AC-12, finds a turd on the seat of his car. Being Billy-no-
mates at work every day is something most of us would struggle
with, even without this level of hostility.

Kate Fleming has the added stress of working as an undercover
officer. Maintaining a false identity to gain the confidence of
suspects who are naturally distrustful is psychologically draining.
That is not to mention the trauma of violence they face. In

Series 2 DI Lindsay Denton, not one to be messed with, pins Kate against a wall and punches her in the abdomen. Kate's undercover hours have wrecked her relationship with the father of her son Josh, and she is separated from husband Mark from Series 2 to 5. When they are reconciled in Series 5, thanks to Kate giving up undercover work, we see they have again split in Series 6. At least she did not pay the ultimate price like DS John Corbett did, murdered by the gang he infiltrated.

Steve Arnott probably makes life more stressful for himself than it needs to be, thanks to his unprofessional indiscretions. He has been exposed for his ill-judged liaisons with colleagues and witnesses, such as nurse Claire Tindall, and even more explosively with DI Lindsay Denton.

In fairness, Steve has suffered more than anyone when it comes to workplace trauma. In Series 1 he is captured and tortured by the OCG – a demonic little Ryan Pilkington almost amputating his fingers.

In Series 4 he is pushed down an office stairwell by one of the "balaclava men", Robert Denmoor. His back is badly damaged and he is initially confined to a wheelchair and struggles to look after himself. By Series 5 he has a painkiller addiction and suffered problems in his sex life with girlfriend DS Sam Railston, caused by his dodgy back. His dependency difficulties get worse by Series 6 when booze is also taking hold. A routine drugs test reveals high levels of analgesics in his body. He is finally forced to get medical help or be suspended.

It is also worth considering the fate of Lindsay Denton, played with grit and intensity by Keeley Hawes across two series. She had a brief relationship with DCC Mike Dryden, became pregnant and was pressured by him into having an abortion. In Series 2 we see that she is having to support her mother, who is in a nursing home. To manage this, Lindsay has sold their home. She accepts a bribe from DS Jayne Akers to protect sexual abuse victim Carly Kirk by ensuring Tommy Hunter is handed to his criminal associates during the convoy ambush. Before she is murdered by DI Matthew Cottan in Series 3, she helps to incriminate the abusers of Danny Waldron and expose Cottan as "the Caddy". She is officially praised for her courageous efforts after her death. However, she is given a cheap local authority funeral, which is entirely unattended by mourners. It is a grim outcome for an officer who, whatever her faults, did more than most to bring down criminal officers.

The most broken we see any of the characters is during Ted Hastings' interrogation by Detective Chief Superintendent Patricia Carmichael in Series 5. Hastings is in the frame for conspiring to murder DS John Corbett. He looks done for as the evidence is laid out against him – disposing of his laptop, making an unofficial visit to OCG man Lee Banks in prison, and the £50k found in his hotel room. Then, finally, the big fella breaks down in tears when he learns that Anne-Marie McGillis, whom he had protected as a young officer in Northern Ireland and who was murdered during the Troubles, was actually Corbett's mother. Tragedy on top of tragedy. Seeing *Line of Duty*'s most charismatic officer distraught is a genuinely painful moment.

However, the personal battles of AC-12's finest are not too distant from the traumas and travails of officers in the real world who take a stand against their bent workmates.

Bitterness, threats and PTSD

While the fictionalised take on anti-corruption work imagined in *Line of Duty* is more lurid than is usually seen in the real world, the truth of how detectives have been afflicted is still bleak and shocking.

Taking on ruthless bent officers damaged many careers. Frank Williamson, Her Majesty's Inspector of Constabulary, resigned in bitterness after being thwarted and sabotaged at every turn while he ran the investigation into *The Times'* allegations about bent detectives in 1969. He was the outsider brought in to see how much truth there was in the charges. He'd had a distinguished career in the provinces, including working as a detective chief superintendent in Manchester, where he had got to know Robert Mark. He was seen at the Home Office as a ruthless and efficient investigator of misconduct, but he was not given sufficient powers to take on the corrupt networks.

Williamson saw clearly how entrenched corruption was in the Met. However, once DI Bernard Robson and DS Gordon Harris were jailed for corruption as a result of their exposure in *The Times*, Williamson knew the corruption spread much further and his attempts to get the evidence had been sabotaged by DCS Bill Moody and others.

Williamson fell into a slough of hopeless despair after his experience at the hands of the Scotland Yard establishment. He resigned in 1971, "fed up with banging his head against a brick wall". This was 11 years before he needed to retire, and he is thought to have done so despite the fact that he would probably have become Her Majesty's Chief Inspector with a far greater pension and likely knighthood. Robert Mark tried to talk him out of it, without success. "He had had enough," Mark said later, "and it says much of the conditions under which we both laboured that a man of his calibre had reached such a point."

Detective Chief Superintendent Fred Lambert was the man who worked so productively with Williamson in the early stages of the corruption probe, before he was kicked off the inquiry. A Scotland Yard insider cooperating with Williamson could not be tolerated. He was replaced by the super-bent Moody. Lambert's mistake was to help the outsider Williamson in coming close to exposing the hidden and massively lucrative porn racket being run by Moody and his boss, Commander Wally Virgo.

Virgo's version was that Lambert was shifted because he was a drunk, a wreck, a truant. Lambert, after being given a series of non-jobs by Virgo, left the force in 1971.

These are text-book cases in how certain figures within the Met blocked outside scrutiny and sidelined officers seen as disloyal.

Some senior officers were at pains not to be seen as disloyal to colleagues or on the side of anti-corruption investigators. A10's Don Williams asked a commander to suspend an officer in his ranks because the man was a target of A10. The commander was scared to do so.

"I can't do that, Don," the commander said. "You don't know what it's like working here."

Williams asked if it would be better if *he* suspended the officer himself. The grateful commander said, "Yes, you do it."

"That kept him out of the limelight," Williams said. "They were shit-scared what would happen to them. That sort of thing was going on, you know, it was dreadful."

The experiences of DC Lew Tassell and DI Tony Kilkerr revealed how eager young constables were initiated into the ranks of the corrupt against their will and the strain that placed on them. Both had money thrust into their pockets by their bosses. As we have already learned, this happened to Tassell at City of London police and to Kilkerr during his time with the Obscene Publications Squad. Both did not want the money and initially did not know where to turn for support.

The price Tassell paid for agreeing to eventually testify against his bent boss, however, was to live in fear. "I'd sometimes go home and sob," he recalled. His state of mind was not helped by threats from other cops. Anyone stepping out of line had to be made an example of.

"I was concerned for my personal safety," Tassell recalled. "I knew who I was dealing with. I was questioned constantly. One of the officers said, 'Well, is it true, Lew, what we hear about you?' Someone else said, 'Well, he's a grass.' And he said, 'No, I don't think he's a grass, because if what you say is true, he'll be wearing a cement raincoat.' Now that is terrifying."

Despite the intimidation, Tassell testified and his evidence helped to convict DCI Phil Cuthbert.

Before joining City of London CID, John Simmonds had worked with Robert Mark's A10 team. He described the hostility directed at officers who investigated their colleagues: "Other officers wanted to ignore you, they wanted nothing to do with you. They didn't trust you, you were seen as the bad people.

"I was going to work one day and had a windscreen blow in right by Finchley police station. I drove my car into the yard and there were two traffic patrol guys there. One of them said, 'I can help you there, mate.' His mate said, 'Where are you attached?' I said, 'I wish you hadn't asked – A10.' They both said, 'Well, you're on your own,' and they left me to it."

While Simmonds put together the case against Phil Cuthbert, Commander Hugh Moore was also alleged in court to have shared a £20,000 bribe, as mentioned by Cuthbert in secretly taped conversations. However, Cuthbert refused to repeat his comments about Moore in his testimony. Moore denied the claims, calling them rubbish, and he was never prosecuted. In his defence, Cuthbert said he was drunk, trying to discredit what he had said on tape.

The problem for Simmonds was that he had to then carry on serving under Moore at City of London police. "I had to live with him for four years." When Moore found out what Simmonds had done, he gave his subordinate a miserable time on a daily, hourly basis. "Whenever he had the opportunity to snipe at me," Simmonds recalled, "try and catch me out, trip me up, he did his level best. I decided that the job was not big enough for Moore and myself. I was completely and utterly disillusioned and decided it was time for me to get out."

Once again, an officer of integrity who had done a difficult and exemplary job in building a case against a senior corrupt detective, found that his reward was to find his own career undermined. You can nail the bent coppers, but their mates will come for you later.

The harshness of the dilemma confronted by those speaking out against colleagues is that it never gets easier. A report by HM Inspector of Constabulary, highlighted by *The Spectator* magazine in 2015, delivered shocking news. Nearly half of 17,200 officers and staff surveyed said that if they became aware of corruption among their colleagues and then reported it, they did not feel their evidence would be treated in confidence and would fear "adverse consequences".

Adverse consequences were certainly the experience of Jackie Malton, a former detective chief inspector at the Met. "It was this sense of belonging within an institution that is so powerful," she said. "If you're on the outside of that and you challenge it, it's crushing. You just get crushed."

She was posted to West End Central police station on Savile Row. It was reported to her that an inspector, known as a bit of a maverick, was going on drugs raids and planting narcotics on people. The officer was subsequently suspended, investigated and charged.

"That whole process was life-defining," Malton recalled. "I remember walking into West End Central canteen and everybody just stood up and walked out. You were seen as the baddie. That feeling of isolation, there was just nowhere to go. It was the toughest thing and it's madness. You're vilified for doing something that was right. I wanted them to say, 'You did the right thing, Jackie, well done.' They said the opposite. But that feeling of wanting to belong to this huge organisation and wanting them to like me for it was the pain that it caused. They didn't respect me for it, they didn't like me for it. That's what hurt."

What is extraordinary about this devastating experience is that she did not speak to anybody about what had happened or how she was feeling. After she recounted these events on the BBC documentary *Bent Coppers: Crossing the Line of Duty* in 2021, she was contacted by a former police officer colleague.

Speaking to this author, Malton explained what followed: "She just said she felt very, very sad at what I had gone through, and that she didn't realise [it] at the time. She felt guilty. And I said, 'Well, don't feel guilty about it. I chose not to tell you.'

"But when you're in the job, everybody's getting on with their life. And we're getting on with a job. Unless you sit down and explain what's happened, nobody can assimilate anything. How can they? You're just telling them the story. And it doesn't mean anything much to them because they're not there. And it's just, I don't know… I don't think I did tell many people, to be honest.

"It's just so terrible at the time you don't want to be talking about it as well."

Even several decades later, her turmoil is still apparent. People have said to her recently that the whole experience sounded so awful, yet Malton still felt as though it was something that had to be coped with.

"When you're in the culture, you never think it's as awful as other people see it," she says. "So when the programme went out, I just got lots of messages on Twitter and emails from people, supportive messages from people in the police and some not in the police, who had no idea. And it's only when you see it... Because you don't go in there [to film a documentary] and say, *Oh, I think I'm gonna cry in this*, you know, it just catches you."

As a gay woman, Malton needed all her fortitude to build what was a distinguished career. She achieved a lot in the aggressively male, heterosexual worlds of the Fraud Squad and the Flying Squad, as well as during long and difficult inquiries, such as that into the New Cross fire of 1981, in which 13 young black people died. Scriptwriter Lynda La Plante used Malton as the inspiration for Jane Tennison in ITV's long-running hit drama *Prime Suspect*.

In addition to helping with *Prime Suspect* and many other TV projects since retiring from the police, Malton volunteers to help addicts in prison. It is work she understands as someone who turned to Alcoholics Anonymous herself, thanks to the pressures of life in the police.

She was invited recently to talk for a few minutes at a book launch near Scotland Yard. The book was about external trauma and how it affected police officers. "I said, 'I'm just going to talk to you for five minutes about internal trauma,'" Malton says. "And there was a woman doctor that came up to me afterwards and said, 'You know, you've got PTSD. Do you know that?' I said, 'What do you mean?' She said, 'You tell that story of West End Central – you have got PTSD. I am an expert in PTSD.'"

Post-traumatic stress disorder means sufferers can feel the emotional fallout from an experience days, months or even years later.

Malton knows of other officers who have suffered in different ways many years after confronting corruption. She tells of a detective superintendent who in the 1990s arrested some police officers. To this day he cannot face going to any CID functions.

"It's because of what people might think of him," she says, "and that's like, affected him for over 30 years. Too scared to go. And then there's another DCI that reported some corruption, and he had a nervous breakdown. It's because of the stress that the organisation puts on you. You become the one that's the wrong one. It is unbelievable."

She describes the police culture as insular and extremely defensive. "They were loath to work in partnership with other people because of fear. It was so white and male. They were fearful of any diversity; they were fearful of black people because they did not understand them, gay people because they didn't understand them. And so in a way, it is a point at which you accept it because the organisation is far too big for you to make any impact on it at all in those areas.

"It's like trying to turn the Titanic; it is an institution, and they're very slow to change. And you just have to accept that you're the oddball, that you've done the right thing, but obviously in this organisation they didn't like you doing the right thing. And it's only years later that people go, 'Oh, my god. This is just outrageous.' And you kind of go, 'Well, it's not that outrageous.'

"But it is! Of course it is. It is outrageous, don't get me wrong, but you were fighting a losing battle. There was nobody you could turn to."

Other former detectives have also felt that successfully exposing corruption could have had an adverse effect on their careers. Don Williams, who was enlisted by Assistant Commissioner Gilbert Kelland to play a leading role in investigating the Porn Squad, said Deputy Assistant Commissioner Ron Steventon warned him about how the anti-corruption squad's successful investigations might be perceived by some in the Scotland Yard hierarchy: "He

[Steventon] said, 'What you've done to the Metropolitan Police, mate, you'll get nothing now.' I thought, *Shit. He's right. That's the first time anybody's said that to me.*"

Williams also thought his boss Kelland, with his success in overseeing the long and painstaking Porn Squad inquiry that saw Cdr Ken Drury and DCS Bill Moody sent to jail, had not been recognised for his work.

"Gilbert Kelland is one of the few ACCs not to be knighted," said Williams. "Why? Because he'd done a job and he'd done it straight. And unfortunately, it brought the job into disrepute, and the politicians and the Home Office mandarins didn't want that.

"I do feel Gilbert was very badly treated. Gilbert Kelland was dead straight, did the job properly, got nothing."

Why would anyone do this job?
Fine officers having their careers curtailed or ended, breakdowns, trauma.

The cost of testifying against colleagues and taking the lead in a corruption case can be huge. Many former corruption investigators spoken to by this author say much of the work in such probes is in reality routine, repetitive and fairly dull. Confirming details, cross-checking statements, locating witnesses. Every now and again, however, one officer had to take responsibility for actioning corruption charges or testifying against a close colleague. That's when the retaliation could be unforgiving.

Line of Duty portrays the harsh price that Hastings, Arnott and Fleming pay in storylines across the six series. Being a fictional drama, the series of course goes to the limit in depicting how some characters end up paying with their lives. Where Hastings, Arnott and Fleming are beset by violence, relationship breakdowns or addiction, the likes of Lindsay Denton, John

Corbett and Maneet Bindra come to grim ends at the hands of the Organised Crime Group.

Thankfully, real anti-corruption work is rarely lethal (though threats like that of the "cement raincoat" made to Lew Tassell were chilling). Part of the fascination of watching *Line of Duty*, one of the few British television dramas to venture into the world of corruption, is watching people doing a job few of us could live with.

Brutal long hours, threats, risk of addiction, relationship breakdown. What is the attraction of the work? While Jackie Malton was not directly involved in anti-corruption investigations, she did, as we have seen, report wrongdoing and suffered emotionally as a result of the vilification of her fellow officers.

You might expect that she would feel bitter about her time in the Met. So does she look back with positive feelings about her police career?

"Yeah, definitely," she says. "I loved my job. I loved being a detective and I enjoyed meeting all those people. I enjoyed interviewing prisoners; I enjoyed meeting the families. You might meet a chairman of a company one day and then you'd be talking to, you know, the opposite end of the spectrum the next. That's the thing about communication – how you talk to a CEO would not be how you talk to the homeless person. It's about stepping into their shoes for a while.

"You can't just understand life from a cop's point of view. You have to stand in their shoes."

While she saw many things wrong with the police during her career in terms of racism, corruption and sexism, Malton found it was her support network outside of work that gave her the balance she needed.

"If you look at the police today, what the media and society think of the police isn't particularly high. But internally, they're probably more stable, more honest, more transparent, a more open organisation than they've ever been. From my point of view, the 70s, 80s and 90s, it was none of those things. But the stability came from the people outside the police."

By relying on those close to her outside of the police world, she was able to put aside the internal negative aspects of being in the Met. Getting out and investigating crimes became her passion.

"I knew that I would be supported externally. Most of the time, you're investigating crimes, you're out there every day talking to different people. And I loved all that. So it was a job that drove me. And the satisfaction I got from being a detective dealing with the members of the public, with families, was the upbeat of it all."

For those in anti-corruption, there was also the straightforward satisfaction in seeing rotten colleagues face justice. Don Williams had heard colleagues making excuses for bent detectives, with comments such as, "It's not fair, these CID officers, they've got to do these things [bend the rules]."

To which Williams' response is, "You don't know what you're talking about. This has nothing to do with catching criminals. This is all to do with making money out of *not* catching criminals.

"It was so much money that was being made by these bastards, it was amazing. The share-outs, honestly. They'd go around collecting the money and they'd come into the office and the chief inspector or inspector would share it all out, the boss getting the bigger share, you know. I mean, dear god, incredible, absolutely incredible."

Despite the stresses of the work and fact that it may not enhance your career prospects, there would have been great satisfaction at the conclusion of the porn trials in 1977 to see senior officers, such as Bill Moody and Ken Drury, found guilty of corruption at last.

Williams is able to look back on his time with A10 and say, "Well, we got the real villains. We got the commanders and chief superintendents.

"The difference was the Met in 1972 actually did something about it [corruption]. And the results were crime rates were going down and detection rates were going up for a couple of years."

In 2019 the then Met Commissioner Cressida Dick blasted *Line of Duty* for its depiction of "casual and extreme corruption" that, she said, did not reflect accurately on contemporary policing.

A response from David Zinzan, a former detective superintendent in the Met's anti-corruption unit who advised on *Line of Duty* scripts, highlighted an ingredient of the series that helped to make it special.

"Some officers say to me: 'Why is it so negative?' I'd have a different spin on that. I'd say it shows that there is a dedicated force who are there to root corruption out."

Confronting embedded networks of ruthless corrupt officers is a job full of jeopardy and high personal stakes. *Line of Duty* mirrors the real work being done by quiet heroes at often huge personal cost.

Even at their low moments, Hastings and AC-12 keep plugging away. As Hastings says in Series 4, "This is beginning to feel like a life's work."

9 – *Line of Duty*'s biggest mystery

'Jesus, Mary and Joseph and the wee donkey'

The defining mystery of *Line of Duty* was the identity of "H". Creator and writer Jed Mercurio conjured a tantalising talking point that gripped viewers over the course of three whole seasons, culminating in the big reveal in Series 6.

The intrigue played with the major theme that ran throughout the arc of the six series – that of what we might call double-agents, or senior police officers working covertly for the Organised Crime Group. Once again, where *Line of Duty* fictionalises and heightens the theme of criminals in uniform, the drama is ad-libbing on real cases.

"H" was a codename and pseudonym that actually referred to a group of four officers. It was given during DI Matthew Cottan's dying declaration at the end of Series 3. Cottan is under questioning for the murder of Lindsay Denton at AC-12 HQ when he is sprung from the office by a corrupt armed officer in cahoots with the OCG. After a chase, one of his accomplices shoots at an armed Kate Fleming, but Cottan jumps in front of her, shielding her from the bullets. She then shoots the gunman and attempts to question the dying Cottan.

Kate records his final declaration on her phone. He implicates Patrick Fairbank in the Sands View Boys Home abuse scandal, which helps to get the former chief superintendent a 10-year sentence.

It is not until episode 5 of Series 4 that it becomes apparent in body-cam footage taken of the dying Cottan that he was able to indicate that the senior officer in charge of corrupt police on behalf of the OCG was someone whose name began with the letter H.

Jed Mercurio had conveniently supplied an abundance of characters with the initial H to fuel the speculation. Could it be ACC Derek Hilton, found dead at the end of Series 4? Having accused Ted Hastings of being "H", blackmailed Maneet Bindra and manipulated Roz Huntley, he was clearly corrupt. Some viewers suspected Roz Huntley, who also appeared on AC-12's list of possible H-es.

Then there was Hastings himself. A thick file could be compiled of circumstantial evidence making him look ripe as a candidate to have joined the dark side. First, there was his terrible financial situation as a result of his ill-judged property investment in the disastrous Kettle Bell Complex. This certainly clouded his judgement in Series 2, when he initially refused to investigate DCC Mike Dryden because Dryden had offered to keep quiet about his financial blunders and dangled the prospect of future promotion.

Ted also revealed his Masonic loyalty when he shielded the odious former Chief Superintendent Patrick Fairbank from being questioned at his home by Kate and Steve. And was it simply poor judgement that prompted Ted to recruit Matthew "the Caddy" Cottan, Tommy Hunter's right-hand man in Central Police, into the ranks of AC-12? It turned out it was. However, he was soon in the frame again in Series 5 when we saw Ted visiting Lee Banks in Blackthorn prison and disposing of his laptop. The visit to Banks meant Hastings had blown John Corbett's cover, and the undercover man was brutally assassinated as a result. Ultimately, Ted is shown to be guilty of nothing more than duff decision-making, but series writer Jed Mercurio clearly went to great lengths to put his hero – and the viewers – through the wringer.

DCS Lester Hargreaves of the Serious and Organised Crime squad, and another thorn in the side of AC-12, got tongues wagging when he turned up at the Eastfield Police Storage Facility during the OCG's spectacular raid in Series 5. However, he was shot and killed by John Corbett during the robbery and was soon discounted as the top criminal cop inside the force. Corbett had suspected Hargreaves of being "H". However, rather than operating as a main player for the OCG, it turned out semen samples found in cold storage at the Pulton House brothel, where underaged girls were forced to work, included one from Hargreaves. It seemed he, like several others, had been blackmailed into working for the crime syndicate.

Other suspects who appear only as photos on the suspects board included various chief inspectors and superintendents (Michelle Harris, Raymond Hall, Susan Hyde-Albert, Paul Haleton, etc).

By Series 5, however, there was yet a further twist. Although Cottan blinked when Kate said "H" as a possible initial of the culprit's name, Steve Arnott makes a further observation on viewing the body-cam footage. Cottan makes four gripping motions with his hand. Four taps is Morse Code for the letter H, but could also indicate four senior officers in Central Police who were doing the bidding of the gangsters. Those already known to be in league with the OCG were ACC Derek Hilton, Senior Legal Counsel Gill Biggeloe and Cottan himself.

So, who was the fourth person, and did their name begin with "H"? Into this vacuum of ambiguity flooded guesses and theories from viewers and the media alike.

Line of Duty armchair sleuths began to join all manner of dots to try to form a picture of who the heck "H" was. Some wondered if it was one of the female characters who were being placed into positions of authority in order to thwart AC-12. Andrea Wise moved into the office of disgraced Detective Chief Constable Mike Dryden and rarely offered Ted Hastings and AC-12 any support. She constantly downplayed the possibility of corruption in the ranks. She only reluctantly gave AC-12 access to Operation Pear Tree – the secretive report on the Organised Crime Group and John Corbett's undercover role in it. She then removed it from AC-12 so that Ted Hastings could be investigated instead. At the end of Series 6, she told Ted he would have to resign because AC-12 was being disbanded. When it came to being "H", Wise had serious dark-horse potential.

In Series 5, Hastings says of DCS Patricia Carmichael, "That woman has been fast-tracked from day one." Few characters have come as close to destroying Hastings' career as the cold, remorseless Carmichael and her AC-3 team. It is only when Kate and Steve expose Gill Biggeloe's ties with the OCG, and then one of Carmichael's team – PS Tina Tranter, another OCG plant – tries to kill Biggeloe, that Hastings is finally able to clear his name. Among the most relieved that Hastings was innocent was the actor who had made him such a popular character, Adrian Dunbar. He said, "It was a relief for me, as I spent all this time playing this character and I always thought Ted had a sense of duty and a moral core. And to have found out I was this arch villain… I would have been in real difficulty accepting that.

"Jed [Mercurio] is aware of our audience and they know Ted has a sense of moral fortitude. I am glad he came out of it with flying colours."

A few suspicious minds latched on to Kate Fleming. However, much of this was fuelled by a trailer for Series 6.

This looked like a stand-off between Ted, Steve and Kate with armed officers. Hastings is heard shouting through a megaphone, "This is Superintendent Hastings, you'll be treated fairly with the full protection of the law." Kate in particular looks troubled. However, that is all a sleight of the editing. Kate is clean. It would have been one lulu of a twist had she turned out to be the embedded crime chief.

Having Kate or Ted revealed as "H" would have been sensational, but whether it would have been true to the internal motivations of the drama, on the other hand, is questionable. Sometimes an extravagant plot twist can undermine a series' credibility. However, when "H" was finally unmasked at the end of Series 6, his identity and stature turned out to be so underwhelming it had the opposite effect – a sigh that amounted to, "Really, is that it?"

Was there a real "H"?

The man said to have parallelled "H" in real life was Hugh Moore, a commander in the City of London police.

Moore was the third most senior man in the force. It was he who called the pointless scenes-of-crime lecture at Wood Street police station, which required the presence of firearms teams who should have been out on patrol to prevent a lethal armed robbery at the *Daily Mirror* building (see chapter 7). It was obvious that officers there had been diverted from doing their jobs.

Moore prompted a feeling of betrayal in DCI Phil Cuthbert, who turned to his boss, John Simmonds, head of CID in the City of London. This was the conversation (also mentioned in chapter 7) in which Cuthbert asked to speak to Simmonds "on the square", or confidentially, one Freemason to another. Simmonds, however, felt that he could not help to cover up the criminality Cuthbert wanted to discuss and decided to record their chat, which took place in a pub.

It was here that Cuthbert told Simmonds of the money from a spate of unsolved armed robberies in the City of London, the "glamour crime" of the 1970s, being shared by officers meant to be investigating the crimes. As Operation Countryman began to focus on allegations emanating from the robbery spree, Cuthbert feared he was being lined up to be the lone scapegoat for the corruption. Simmonds, who had previously worked for Robert Mark's new anti-corruption squad, A10, said, "I think he was panicking having been told by Hugh Moore that this big inquiry was going to go down and Cuthbert was going to be on his own and be the fall guy, the man blamed for all that had gone on."

According to Cuthbert, Hugh Moore was actually top dog in the City of London's corruption pyramid. Cuthbert revealed that officers shared out £20,000 handed over by criminals to avoid prosecution for one of their robberies (equivalent to £100,000 today). He said to Simmonds that the 1976 armed raid on the *Daily Express* payroll van was a "Hughie Moore job, and he's a greedy bastard, always has been… Hughie had a drink out of that fucking *Daily Express* job."

Simmonds did succeed in gathering enough evidence to support an Old Bailey trial for Cuthbert. While Cuthbert claimed he was drunk when caught on tape implicating Moore, Simmonds had managed to persuade Lew Tassell, who as a young City of London detective had been pressed by Cuthbert into accepting bribes, to testify against his old boss.

In the BBC documentary *Bent Coppers: Crossing the Line of Duty*, Tassell said of his nerve-racking decision to turn whistleblower, "Given the opportunity, I wanted to tell someone. It was a leap of faith in a way. I trusted him [Simmonds] because I knew if I told him that he would do the right thing."

In response, Simmonds said of Tassell, "I believed in his honesty and his integrity, and he agreed to turn witness against what had taken place."

Cuthbert was found guilty of conspiracy to obtain bribes and corruptly presenting evidence in 1982, thanks to their efforts. He was sentenced to three years.

Cuthbert would not repeat in court the comments he had made on tape pointing the finger at Hugh Moore. Simmonds had recorded him saying of his boss, "Hughie's run Bishopgate and half the City's police for years and years and years. He's been the greatest villain unhung ever since."

Moore, despite allegations in court that he shared in the £20,000 bribe, was never prosecuted. Without Cuthbert's testimony, there was a lack of evidence against him. Moore carried on in the police until 1993, driving Simmonds out of the force in the meantime by constantly undermining him in revenge for his exposure of City of London corruption. Moore died of heart failure, aged 64, after trying to arrest someone suspected of being a bogus charity worker.

"There's no doubt about it," said Lew Tassell. "There was one particular person they wanted to catch – Commander Hughie Moore."

Newspapers have speculated that Moore could have been a real-life "H". However, if he was the "greatest villain unhung", there was never enough evidence to charge him – unlike the *Line of Duty* character unmasked in Series 6 as the remaining OCG infiltrator going by that codename.

It was Buckells – mother of god!

Howls of anguish and dismay greeted the revelation that Ian Buckells – yes, that dope! – was "H", or "the Fourth Man", as the high-ranking OCG figure was known by Series 6.

As former Flying Squad officer Jackie Malton, who has advised on television dramas, told this author, "I hated it. I just felt cheated. That ruined it for me. It didn't stop me watching the programme, but I thought that was terrible. He didn't deserve it. There is nothing about the character. There was nothing; he had no charisma. Jed Mercurio [writer and creator] said that was the whole reason for it, but what I would say is that having worked in drama myself over the years, you need to reward the audience. And I felt the audience wasn't rewarded at all."

She was not alone. Media outlets were bombarded with furious comments from viewers. "AC-12? More like Anti-Climax 12," said one. Another fumed, "What a way to end what has been a gripping series from day one... what a huge let down." One outraged fan invoked the spirit of Ted Hastings on Facebook: "The wee donkey could have written a better ending."

When listings magazine *Radio Times* ran a poll asking viewers if they had been satisfied by the Buckells revelation, 17 per cent said yes, while 83 per cent gave it the thumbs down.

Line of Duty has stirred several controversies in its 10 years, but, with millions glued to their screens for the big finale, this was probably the biggest.

What caused the upset? It is correct to say that Buckells has no charisma. He is throughout the six series a dunderhead, dull and dour. As Malton put it, there is nothing about him.

Or so it seemed.

Many devotees were expecting one of the series' big beasts to be unmasked. Ted Hastings would have been a rather controversial choice. Marcus Thurwell – who we only saw in a photograph – was a new figure of suspicion in Series 6. As a senior investigator he was connected to a number of scandalous cases, including the Lawrence Christopher murder and Sands View Boys Home abuse scandal. Of course, Thurwell is dead, having apparently burned to death in his Spanish villa. But then people have appeared to be dead before in *Line of Duty* (Roz Huntley looked deceased – until she rose up to kill her attacker, Tim Ifield).

Philip Osborne, who becomes the new Chief Constable of Central Police at the end of Series 6, was also put forward in some quarters as the Fourth Man. Right from Series 1 he was on the wrong side of right, pressuring Steve Arnott to help cover up the killing by police of an innocent civilian.

Some viewers wondered whether Steve Arnott was the OCG's insider. Meanwhile, the bookies had Patricia Carmichael as the 2/1 favourite, followed by Philip Osborne, Hastings, Thurwell, Jo Davidson and Andrea Wise, with Buckells as the 16/1 outsider.

It is something of a convention in fiction, drama and movies that the one whodunit is usually devilishly clever, personable and often a bit of an anti-hero. Think Walter White in *Breaking Bad* or Wendy Byrde in *Ozark*. These characters are so bad they're good. We root for them.

Buckells, on the other hand, put the plodding into Plod. Craig Parkinson, the actor who played "Dot" Cottan, summed up the detective most succinctly on his podcast *Obsessed with... Line of Duty* – "Buckells is a wally." He was easily overlooked in all the hype around the show. But Jed Mercurio was adamant that the Fourth Man should be a character who had been in the action from the very first series. Which Buckells was, but most viewers and critics overlooked him despite subtle clues along the way.

We discover in Series 1 that as a young detective constable Buckells was part of the team looking into the racially motivated murder of Lawrence Christopher. Buckells' bosses on that case were the well-bent Marcus Thurwell and suspected-dodgy Philip Osborne. Tip-offs and forensic leads were not followed up, while investigative foot-dragging meant the gang members suspected of a racist attack were all released without charge. It turns out Thurwell sabotaged the case to shield gang member Darren Hunter, son of Tommy Hunter, OCG boss. Quite the education for the young detective constable, who it appears was recruited to this rotten squad thanks to his Masonic contacts (which are always ominous in the *Line of Duty* universe).

Also in the first series, Buckells, by now an inspector, is assigned to investigate the disappearance of businesswoman Jackie Laverty by CS Derek Hilton, himself exposed in Series 4 as the OCG's high-ranking puppet in Central Police. The two men are on familiar first-name terms with each other. In the first of his many lacklustre inquiries, Buckells interviews the nasty juvenile Ryan Pilkington, the BMX courier for the OCG. It was Buckells' decision not to charge Pilkington, so that later, when grown-up Ryan applies to join the police, he has a clean record to help him get through the background checks. Odd, too, that Buckells never spots that PC Pilkington is probably an OCG criminal in uniform on reacquaintance with him during Series 6.

After Tommy Hunter's arrest, Buckells lets Matthew Cottan – Hunter's secret frontman in the police – have a private chat with the gang boss. This allowed Cottan to warn Hunter to go into witness protection. More blundering by Buckells, or something more suspicious?

He does not appear in Series 2 and 3, but when Buckells finally turns up in Series 4, he has climbed the ranks, the implication being that the mediocre detective's rise has been enabled by fellow bent officers. One former Met detective told this author: "You used to see people get things [promotions] and think, *Well, how the bloody hell did he get that job?* You know, he's absolutely useless." Then it emerges that the appointee and those that recommended him are in the same Masonic lodge. This kind of realistic detail helps to add credibility to Mercurio's decision to make Buckells the Fourth Man. Sometimes bent officers do lack charisma and outstanding ability. Their rise up the ranks is down to the contacts they have, who they can be useful to.

Actor Nigel Boyle's performance captures perfectly Buckells' gormless but boastful character. It is hard not to cringe at the injustice of his good fortune when the detective, now with the rank of chief inspector, replaces DCI Roz Huntley as boss of Operation Trapdoor. Plum jobs just keep falling his way.

He spots Kate Fleming working undercover on Huntley's team, who he of course remembers from earlier encounters. Hastings orders him not to blow her cover. Buckells pulls a sour face but agrees, though he refuses to hand over intel on a meeting because he says he is "no grass". The sharpness in the writing here is that Buckells' duplicity is easily misread as smarmy self-righteousness.

When Kate is exposed as an AC-12 spy, Buckells denies it is his doing. Hastings vents his anger on him, to which the spiteful DCI replies, "You lot treat everyone like mugs. Who's the mug now?" Again, Buckells reveals how small-minded and spiteful he is – surely, no match for Hastings and AC-12.

Buckells continues his irresistible rise while off-stage during Series 5. While the undeserving detective is being promoted to detective superintendent, AC-12 moves on from "H" to the theory of "the Fourth Man". Three members of the bent "H" quartet had been outed – Cottan, Biggeloe and Hilton. As viewers started speculating about who the fourth members was, showrunner Jed Mercurio pulled a nifty piece of misdirection by not having Buckells in Series 5 at all.

In Series 6, Detective Superintendent Ian Buckells returns, this time as guv'nor to Kelly Macdonald's DCI Jo Davidson. In that role, he was in overall charge of Operation Lighthouse, the investigation into the murder of journalist Gail Vella. Surprise, surprise – with Buckells calling the shots, the case remained unsolved.

He was instrumental in delaying the arrest of suspect Ross Turner, saying he was doubtful about the validity of a tipoff and the team should wait for executive sign-off. By the time the raid on Turner's accommodation went ahead, Turner had scarpered and officers found Terry Boyle installed there instead. Hastings accuses him of being a decision-dodger – but again, Buckells' failure masks his double-dealing.

This crafty operator then backs the arrest of Terry Boyle, a vulnerable adult with Down's syndrome, for Vella's murder. Boyle is an ideal patsy, fitting the misguided theory of a "lone stalker" and helping to deflect the investigation away from the OCG. Buckells also manages to expose the Covert Human Intelligence Source – CHIS – who can identify whether Boyle is the man who had been bragging about killing the journalist. The CHIS is a sex worker called Alastair Oldroyd – who promptly turns up dead. More spiffy police work from Buckells.

It would appear that series writer Jed Mercurio may not be a fan of the golf scene. The sport seems to symbolise all that is suspicious in the *Line of Duty* world of policing. It began with the arrest of Tommy Hunter at the Edge Park Golf Club, followed by his reference to "the best caddy I ever had", who turned out to be Cottan, the caddy he groomed to be his cop insider. Then, lo and behold, sharp-eyed viewers spotted golf clubs in Buckells' office, as well as in the boot of his car, lying next to missing Operation Lighthouse case files. His office is also decorated with photos of himself on the fairways. Golf is used as an ideally clubbable setting for Buckells to move in the wrong circles.

Buckells puts OCG man Ryan Pilkington up for a commendation after the fatal reservoir car plunge. Kate compliments Davidson for getting Pilkington into her squad, to which Davidson responds, "That was Buckells' idea. Family friend or something. Probably got a nudge down at the Masonic lodge." Freemasonry, like golf, always raises suspicions. It also should have been suspected by now that Buckells must have had a good idea who Pilkington really was and to whom he was loyal.

In the third episode of Series 6, Hastings finally gets to arrest Buckells. This is because of those missing Lighthouse files and his questionable links with a so-called witness, Deborah Devereux, who it turned out owed Buckells a debt of gratitude. Buckells had got her off an assault charge in the past and she had now conveniently turned up claiming knowledge implicating Terry Boyle in Vella's murder.

Many viewers no doubt felt that blundering Buckells had finally been exposed for his shoddy police work. But few would have suspected him, even at this stage, of being a vital OCG operator. One fan Tweeted: "Buckells couldn't run a bath, let alone an OCG." Many may have assumed that Jo Davidson had actually dropped Buckells into Hastings' lap. When confronted with evidence of his manoeuvrings in the deaths of hitman Carl Banks, informant Alastair Oldroyd and PC Lisa Patel (drowned by Pilkington in episode 3), Buckells plays dumber than dumb: "I don't know why I don't know." Even DCS Patricia Carmichael is taken in by his trademark incompetence and drops the charges against him. To top it all, Buckells is not only a blunderer but lazy too. When Jo Davidson says one evening she has no update on the case for him, he moans, "I should have been back home ages ago with my feet up."

A chilling sign of his OCG credentials, however, comes during his incarceration in HMP Blackthorn. Buckells is present in the cell with convicted lawyer Jimmy Lakewell when Lee Banks enters and garrots Lakewell. This was clearly a warning to the quivering Buckells to remember where his allegiances lay.

Once charges against Buckells were dropped, Jo Davidson gets a message on her computer from the "Unknown User" who issues her orders from the OCG. This time she is instructed to get rid of Kate Fleming. With hindsight, this looks very much like Buckells finally venting his longstanding dislike of the AC-12 investigator and the threat she presents to him.

In the end it is Buckells' self-importance and hubris that get the better of him. During his episode 7 grilling, he at first resorts to eye-rolling and no-comments. It is the infamous misspelling of "definately" that points the finger at Buckells. This has been previously noted in online communications between the OCG and John Corbett, then in an order from a Spanish IP address stating that Jo Davidson needed to be silenced.

AC-12 find that same spelling error in Buckells' handwritten reports and he is hauled into the glass box for questioning. It is only when an exasperated Ted Hastings refers to his corruption and incompetence, calling him a "blundering fool", that Buckells can no longer resist saying with a disdainful smirk, "Yeah, right. I'm a blundering fool? I'm only the one who's made total mugs out of you lot."

His mask has finally slipped. The bumbling detective in the "crap suits" has been leading a double life. He had properties worth £3 million and tax-haven bank accounts tucked away all the time.

Showrunner Jed Mercurio explained why they had gone for Buckells. "We decided pretty early that it wasn't going to be Hastings," he said, "because that doesn't make any sense, but then there were lots of other candidates who potentially it could have been.

"We weighed up what we wanted to say dramatically. By going for this crossover between incompetence and corruption, rather than a criminal mastermind, it was a down ending. But it couldn't be a predictable solution."

The production team knew Buckells would be controversial, but they also wanted it to be a well-crafted surprise. The audience reaction was real shock, and Mercurio added, "I guess some people had strident reactions against what it said about the nature of corruption."

The howls of derision that greeted Buckells' exposure carried real disappointment for many viewers. One Tweeter asked his followers, "Did it hurt? When you gave 10 years of your life to *Line of Duty* only for H to be Ian Buckells?"

Even actor Nigel Boyle was stunned to discover the character he had been playing was it. "I never suspected it because I know how Jed [Mercurio] leads people down the garden path with really good red herrings," he said in interviews after the finale was shown. "So I didn't really pay too much attention to things like Buckells' golf clubs etc, but clearly I should have done.

"I'd fully bought in to the idea that Buckells was low on competence levels, but, looking back, it all makes sense."

Some viewers, however, had worked out that the buck did not stop with Buckells. He was not the puppet master we were led to think "H" was. He was a mediocre middleman with friends in all the corrupt places. Bumptious, boring and second-rate, he still managed to slide relentlessly up the greasy pole of promotion because he was always a useful tool (pun intended) for the real crime bosses. The man could not close an investigation or even spell, but failing upwards came easily.

Hastings pinpoints Buckells' motivation: "Over the years, we've investigated all manner of motives, but the basest, most mundane of all is plain, simple greed."

This is actually something of a departure for *Line of Duty*. Most characters who have gone over to the dark OCG side, or were being set up by the OCG for future manipulation, have been compromised in some way. PC Hari Bains (gambling problems), DCC Mike Dryden (sexual encounter), Vihaan Malhotra (gambling problems), DCS Lester Hargreaves (sexual encounter), Sgt Jane Cafferty (affair), DCI Tony Gates (DNA taken and planted on Jackie Laverty's body), and PC Maneet Bindra (her cousin, Vihaan, is a gambler) were all coerced, or had the potential to be coerced, by the crime group. Efforts were also made to suborn two of *Line of Duty*'s most compelling characters, DI Lindsay Denton and DCI Roz Huntley, into the OCG orbit by luring them into breaking the law.

Others, such as Ryan Pilkington and Matthew Cottan, were placed into the police to purposely work on behalf of criminals. Such infiltrators are called sleepers, and while their occurrence is far less common than straightforward greed, they do exist. One former detective told this author that he had been involved in an investigation using phone intercepts. They picked up a conversation in which a former officer in Essex said to a criminal target being monitored, "Right, I'm in the Met now. What do you want me to do?" The officer was clearly working with the criminal under surveillance.

So, Cottan and Pilkington are all too believable as characters infiltrated into Central Police. However, it is the blackmailing of officers that is often repeated throughout the drama, which is one area in which *Line of Duty* does not reflect the real world to an accurate degree. That is not to say that officers are never blackmailed, but inducement and greed are far more common causes of corruption, and Buckells is the show's one major example of pure avarice driving corruption.

He is one of the only characters who is blatantly in it for the riches on offer. Let's face it, he's got little else going for him. That makes him a strong reflection of how corruption commonly occurs in the real world.

The fact that he is an uninspiring personality – which clearly riled many viewers – is also close to the truth. In large institutions such as Central Police in *Line of Duty* – or the Met in real life – cream does not always rise to the top. This is particularly true when there are networks of bent bosses offering a "drink" to young recruits. For every detective of the calibre of Kate Fleming, there are others like Ian Buckells, happy to take the backhanders and any advancement on offer from other bent officers or mates down the lodge.

Jed Mercurio said when *Line of Duty* launched in 2012 that while he valued television drama as escapism, he also thought there was room for it "to examine our institutions in a more forensic light". In Ian Buckells, he showed how corruption often works – stealthily, brutally, fronted by charmless mediocrities.

And with the whole saga of "H", Mercurio shifted the sands repeatedly. "H" was not one person but four. The Fourth Man was not the mastermind but just another conduit to the OCG.

Adrian Dunbar hinted on the red carpet at the 2021 Baftas, "There may be a way to go with all that [the question of "H"]. We don't know yet, do we? There are rumours. Who knows?"

Buckells was in plain sight from Series 1, but his exposure at the end of Series 6 felt like the end of a long story arc. So, if not Buckells, then who was pulling his and the OCG's strings?

It's perfectly set up for another instalment.

10 - Making a Mark – 478 officers removed

'Now we're sucking diesel'

The real Ted Hastings – getting the job done

Robert Mark made genuine breakthroughs against entrenched networks of corruption and a Met culture of complacency. He is still lauded today as a no-nonsense Commissioner who showed that it was possible to confront and amputate from the force those officers bent on lining their pockets or subverting the law.

It is no wonder he is held up as the inspiration for Ted Hastings. In addition to bloody-minded confrontations with corrupt officers, however, the two figures have another factor in common. While both achieved successes against the forces of anti-justice, neither could claim, of course, that they had wiped out malfeasance once and for all.

Mark made a promising start. He knew the public would never believe in the police if they could not see that the Met was accountable. Complacent he was not. Where serious allegations were made, these would be backed up with time-consuming criminal investigations and prosecutions where deemed appropriate. The next line of defence against bent coppers was staunch use of the force's internal disciplinary procedures, which could lead to various sanctions, including the sack.

The landmark success during Mark's time as Commissioner – and the most glaring departure with the complacent past – was the trials of senior members of the so-called Dirty Squad (the Obscene Publications Squad – OPS). These took place between November 1976 and June 1977 and were the result of a three-year probe by the Serious Crime Squad, which had some crossover with Mark's new A10 unit. The old days of generally avoiding admitting to and dealing with wrongdoers in the police seemed to be over. The investigation was long and painstaking, and resulted in a series of high-profile Old Bailey trials. Mark wanted justice for the Dirty Squad to be done and to be seen by the public, and it was.

This time it was not the odd officer who was scapegoated. The major players were convicted. These included DCS Bill Moody and Cdr Wally Virgo, who each received a 12-year sentence, though Virgo's conviction was subsequently quashed on appeal (on the grounds that the trial judge did not direct the jury properly). Cdr Ken Drury got eight years.

At the earlier corruption trial in 1972 that resulted from the allegations in *The Times*, it was an inspector and sergeant – Bernard Robson and Gordon Harris – that were caught and found guilty. Moody had successfully sabotaged all attempts to prove that corruption was spread far wider than these two. The damage to the corrupt network was contained to just Robson and Harris.

In the Dirty Squad trials, on the other hand, Moody and Drury were among a group of very senior men who were pursued and charged. Moody in particular was at the hub of an efficient corruption web that raked in tens of thousands of pounds in return for licensing and ensuring the smooth running of Soho's illicit porn racket. He also wielded far-reaching power, ensuring the names of major porn dealers did not appear in OPS files. He was able to ruthlessly remove young officers who opposed the corruption from his squad, and discredit senior men, such as DCS Fred Lambert, who attempted to investigate it. However, as men such as Moody and Drury, and many others, were locked up, it was no longer possible to downplay corruption as the odd "rotten apple". In addition to them, 18 officers from the rank of constable to commander (including three inspectors) were sentenced to more than 100 years in prison. Robert Mark effectively lifted the lid on how deep and insidious police criminality was. Having exposed the Met's dirty linen to public scrutiny, he then started cleaning it up.

Mark would write of the Dirty Squad trials in his autobiography: "This ended the 'firm within a firm' of which *The Times* had complained, which in its heyday had made thousands of pounds a year from pornography. Their immunity for so long was an indication of the extent of corruption within the detective branch, which was not, of course, limited to pornography. The case illustrates dramatically the need for the sweeping changes in organisation and control in 1972, which made continuance or repetition of such wrongdoing not merely less likely but, once disclosed, virtually certain to bring swift retribution."

In all, Mark's reforms, including setting up the anti-corruption unit A10, flushed out 478 officers following or in anticipation of criminal or disciplinary proceedings. Seventy-six went through formal proceedings, 50 of them being prosecuted. So, 402 facing allegations had therefore probably anticipated they would not be exonerated and instead resigned. If dodgy officers could not be prosecuted, Mark ensured the full weight of internal disciplinary procedures were thrown at them. Some were dismissed, others might be offered early retirement packages on the grounds of "ill health". The objective was to get the bad officers out the door.

Departures under the old regime had averaged just 16 a year. During Marks' four years and 11 months in charge, the average was closer to 100 a year.

Ridding the Met of criminal officers made the force more effective in fighting crime. The year 1974 saw crime rates rising, but CID were arresting more suspects than ever. There were 98,000 arrests that year, 11 per cent up on the previous year. Mark felt that showed morale was good, that kicking out bent officers had the tacit support of policemen and women who were devoted to doing the job conscientiously.

Bank robberies were on a downward trajectory, from 65 in 1972 to 26 in 1973 and 17 in 1974. A newly formed Robbery Squad was making good progress, with 150 suspects arrested for robberies dating back to 1965. "However, a number of those faced with honest and trustworthy detectives for the first time in their experience, began to sing," Mark wrote. "The age of the supergrass had arrived."

The Drug Squad was replaced by the Central Drugs and Illegal Immigration Unit, which was attempting to restore relations with HM Customs and Excise, which had grown to distrust the Met's detectives. Elsewhere, the Flying Squad, Regional Crime Squad and Serious Crime Squad were all "achieving success on a scale never before experienced," said Mark, "largely because at long last they enjoyed the trust of CID, uniformed and provincial colleagues alike".

Finally, in a flourish that might astonish 21st century Met commissioners, Mark would cite national opinion polls showing that in the latter period of his time in charge, the police enjoyed more confidence and respect than any other organisation or profession.

Mark was by no means perfect, but he was brought in at a time when the Met was besieged by outrageous corruption scandals, and in true Ted Hastings style, he did not shirk the trouble he faced.

Like Ted Hastings, Robert Mark had his opponents

Robert Mark retired in 1977. Part of the reason for his departure was the 1976 Police Act, which included provisions to introduce an element of civilian scrutiny of police disciplinary hearings. He did not object to independent scrutiny, just the way the Act provided it.

It is ironic that it was political support from Home Secretaries and the Home Office that propelled provincial outsider Mark to take control and carry out his reforms, but he later felt compelled to leave the job as a result of government actions.

In the fictional world of *Line of Duty*, it is hard not to resist a comparison with anti-corruption chief Ted Hastings at the end of Series 6. He too has overcome sniping and embedded opposition to expose corruption. The four prime OCG operatives who infiltrated the police – Matthew Cottan, Derek Hilton, Gill Biggeloe and Ian Buckells – have been exposed and dealt with.

And yet despite his successes, senior figures in policing and politics have turned against AC-12. Hastings is told that owing to budget issues, his unit is to be merged with sister squads AC-3 and AC-9, with the budget being hacked by 90 per cent.

Oh, and there is no place for Ted in the new team. Thank you and good riddance.

Robert Mark's departure was not so ignominious. He had been knighted in 1973 and his anti-corruption reforms are still lauded today. But he did not get everything right, and he had his detractors.

In April 1972, he had first addressed CID with his uncompromising remarks: "I told them they represented what had long been the most routinely corrupt organisation in London, that nothing and no one would prevent me from putting an end to it…"

There was no question that the new Commissioner came out all guns blazing. In his autobiography, Mark quoted Macbeth in the chapter about how he tackled corruption: "If it were done when 'tis done, then 'twere well it were done quickly."

Macbeth is talking, of course, about assassination, but clearly Mark felt taking on CID required a comparable level of grit and resolution. He confronted the detectives quickly and ruthlessly – something he later felt he had slightly misjudged.

"On reflection," he wrote, "I am sorry that I did not make the point that the great majority of the CID must not only have been honest but anxious for reform. Were that not so, reform would clearly have been impossible. It could not have been achieved without the wide measure of support it was given by the CID generally."

However, he certainly riled some officers. Dick Kirby met Robert Mark on the day he joined the Metropolitan Police, 10 July 1967, at Peel House basic training centre in London. He would subsequently spend much of his career with Scotland's Serious Crime Squad and the Flying Squad. At the time, Mark was Assistant Commissioner for D department and gave Kirby and his classmates a pep talk.

Kirby accepts that Mark was good at communicating with the media and not slow to speak out against bad practices. Moreover, there were plenty of honest cops who, like Mark, wanted to see the "small corrupt cadre of senior officers" eradicated. "But he went about it the wrong way, like an avenging angel wielding a flaming sword, and tarred all CID officers with the same brush," Kirby told this author. "By the time he realised that all CID officers were not corrupt, it was too late. The damage was done."

A particular criticism of Kirby's is that many officers recruited to A10, Mark's independent investigators of corruption allegations, were just not up to the job. They had "never confronted an angry man in their lives", but the implied power of having the title of detective went to their heads. If unable to mount criminal prosecutions against detectives, they resorted to using the Police Discipline Code against them, which could result in anything from a fine to dismissal. The influx of new faces simply did not have the skill set or long-honed insight of established CID officers.

"With Mark's A10 department, just by putting the sobriquet 'detective' in front of one's rank, it doesn't mean that one will become a detective; in the same way that donning a 10-gallon hat won't turn the wearer into an authentic cowboy," was Kirby's pithy analogy.

It was not just in the junior ranks that Mark undermined Scotland Yard's investigative capability. Kirby's view was that, "The role of Assistant Commissioner (Crime) – the man in charge of all London's detectives – went to Gilbert Kelland, who had spent all of his 30-plus years' service in uniform. Decent enough, but an uninformed dope."

Defenders of Mark and Kelland would no doubt counter Kirby's criticism by pointing out that Kelland led the three-year Porn Squad investigation that resulted in the conviction of senior officers, such as DCS Bill Moody and Cdr Ken Drury.

Mark's aim, according to Kirby, was to destroy CID. He cites the practice Mark introduced of interchange, whereby a detective constable who passed the sergeant's exam would then be returned to uniform. He might later make it back into CID, but that was not guaranteed. Other ranks faced the same process. This diluted the investigative talent pool, in Kirby's view.

"Over the years, Scotland Yard – who had once been the western world's premier flagship for criminal investigation – crumbled until it has become the shabby joke that it is today," Kirby told this author. "A chronic lack of leadership, detectives who can't detect, crime rampant and offences which not only go undetected, they're seldom investigated in the first place.

"And the fault for this pathetic state of affairs, I lay at Mark's door."

Kirby is today a crime historian and author of several books on policing and crime. "You may come to the conclusion that I was a bitter officer, passed over for promotion, sent back to uniform, demoted – but if so, you'd be wrong," he said. "I loved the Metropolitan Police, especially the CID, where I spent practically all of my service; and although I was subjected to a number of malicious complaints by disgruntled armed robbers, I emerged unscathed – unlike so many who fell by the wayside, thanks to the dictums of Mark and his myrmidons."

One aspect of this critique, with which another former detective, Brian Pender, concurs, is elevating the uniformed branch to such an extent.

"I think that putting the uniform department in charge of the CID was not a good move in the long term," he told this author. "It might have been needed in the short term. But it weakened CID."

However, he was solidly on the side of Mark overall, saying his confrontation with corrupt officers was made necessary by those in CID who had disgraced the Met.

Pender said Mark had a big effect on his career. "What Mark did was he gave us the confidence to join the CID. I was invited to join CID before Mark came. I didn't want to know."

The stories he had heard about CID had put him off the detective branch. There was no specific incident or experience that deterred him, but things he heard.

"Innuendo, canteen gossip," he said. "It was the general drift of conversation that made me think, *I don't want to belong to this at the moment.* The idea of corruption just never occurred to me, until I entered the police service and began to hear about things."

Mark's arrival was welcomed by Pender's contemporaries in uniform and younger CID officers, "but certainly not among the older generation".

There were several reasons why Mark was welcomed. "He came to London," Pender says, "from Leicester with a great reputation. And also because his remit was to dig out corruption, seek out corrupt police officers and make sure that they left the police service or were prosecuted if there was sufficient evidence.

"Over the years, going back to the 60s, 70s and 80s, the public were not inclined to convict police officers. There had to be overwhelming evidence to convict a police officer of corruption, and juries were not inclined to do that because of the bond that existed between the public and the police. But, of course, the other side of the coin is that corrupt detectives are invariably very clever, switched-on, crafty people. And it takes a lot to nail them down.

"Robert Mark very much addressed the symptoms of the problem."

Pender met Mark when he was a young constable on the occasion of his receiving the Chief Constable of Leicester's award for arresting two murderers from Leicester. He went on to serve in the Flying Squad.

"I don't think any of the modern-day commissioners, other than maybe Peter Imbert and to a lesser extent Paul Condon, can come anywhere near Robert Mark," Pender said.

"Mark was a straight talker. And he wouldn't take any nonsense from anybody, not even politicians. He was not a politician. He was a policeman. And he was not prepared to play politics. He stood by the police officers too. A lot of people didn't like him – it's not so much that they were crap, but they were frightened as, goodness, he entered the police service like a hurricane."

Jackie Malton, formerly of the Flying Squad, joined Leicester police in 1970, shortly after Mark moved to Scotland Yard.

She said, "I just thought he was a man of complete integrity. 'The police should catch more criminals than it employs' – that's what he said. He was a great reformer.

"I think he was one of those that did look at the time to improve race relations with communities in London. He was open, and I think that's what the police needs. It can't be defensive. He was an iconic commissioner."

Many former detectives would argue that Mark did not suffer the same level of political meddling that modern commissioners experience.

Malton felt it was indicative of how challenging the job had become that there was no stampede of candidates putting themselves forward to replace Cressida Dick as Commissioner, a job that eventually went to Sir Mark Rowley.

"You have people like Priti Patel, Sadiq Khan, Boris Johnson – you know that you're just a puppet, an absolute puppet. They will always blame the police. So you have a thankless task."

When asked what is needed today to sort out the Met's many scandals, former A10 detective Don Williams says succinctly, "Robert Mark."

He adds, "Well, he's the man, he sorted them all. And that's why there's so many dislike him. I went to his funeral and there were about six people there. And the Yard had sent a colour party down, but that's all that were there, because some of the CID still disliked him, because of what he did to them. And what he did to them… they bloody well asked for it."

Ex-Met detective George Thomson-Smith also admired the forthright way in which Mark oversaw sensational operations, such as the 1975 Spaghetti House siege in Knightsbridge, London. This lasted five days when three armed robbers took the staff down into a basement storeroom and barricaded themselves in. It ended with the hostages released unharmed and the armed robbers imprisoned.

Of Mark's anti-corruption reforms, Thomson-Smith said, "He introduced changes at a fantastic speed. He led in a very confident way, was very direct."

His legacy

Sir Robert Mark died in 2010.

He stirred up controversies with his trenchant views. He outraged the legal profession with his criticisms of certain unscrupulous defence lawyers. He infuriated many in CID with his bloody-minded expressions of condemnation against its worst elements – a move he realised was perhaps too offensive to many decent detectives who felt blamed unfairly.

He has been accused of favouring a paramilitary style of policing. This is based not just on his promotion of the uniformed branch at the expense of the CID. Having experienced a range of wartime roles and theatres of combat, he expanded the role of the Special Patrol Group, which was subsequently accused of brutality against protestors, even the deaths of a couple of them. Though sometimes praised by liberals for his campaign against corruption, he was no liberal. He criticised the National Council for Civil Liberties as well as the BBC or publications that focused on police corruption or racism. Mark was on the wrong side of history when he praised police having to contend with a demonstration on behalf of the Shrewsbury pickets, "less attractive adherents of the Labour movement". A group of trade unionists known as the "Shrewsbury 24" were sent to jail during trials in 1973 and 1974 after a building workers' strike in 1972, for offences including conspiracy to intimidate and affray. After 47 years, the convictions were quashed in 2021 when the Court of Appeal finally ruled them unsafe.

One final criticism was that while his reforms sought to demonstrate that the police could be trusted to seriously look into allegations of dishonesty, they were still policing themselves (A10 and its successors continued a system of internal police scrutiny). His opposition to the Police Act 1976, over which he resigned, was motivated by the proposal within it to shift ultimate responsibility for investigating complaints against the police away from deputy chief officers in favour of a new Police Complaints Board, consisting of civilian members nominated by the Prime Minister. In the event, the bill was watered down and deputy chief officers remained in charge of complaints. However, A10 ceased to exist at Scotland Yard and was replaced by a Complaints Investigation Bureau (CIB). Not until the establishment in 2004 of the Independent Police Complaints Commission (IPCC, consisting of 18 non-police members) would there be external accountability – 175 years after the Met was set up. In all that time, the police investigated themselves.

However, whatever the criticisms of some former CID officers and commentators in the intervening years, Mark's achievement in stripping away Scotland Yard's complacency and bad practice when dealing with corruption allegations has secured him an unimpeachable place in Met history.

His successor, Sir David McNee, did not shine in the role, while some others have stepped down early faced with controversy – all of which helps Robert Mark to stand out. *The Guardian*'s obituary encapsulated his career like this: "Mark remains probably the most accomplished postwar commissioner."

The Official Encyclopedia of Scotland Yard stressed how much he changed the role of Commissioner: "He will be remembered first and foremost as the commissioner who ensured that none of his successors could overlook the need for constant vigilance inside the force to discover and discipline policemen who allow apparently unimportant departures from perfect practice to grow into complacent malpractice and confident corruption. In the public eye, he was the man who cleaned up the Met."

Mark's time in office as Britain's most powerful policeman was a break with the past. He stirred up opposition by no longer allowing the Yard's senior figures to gloss over wrongdoing in the CID or permitting that branch immunity from outside scrutiny. From then on, Met Commissioners would not be able to defend the old ways again.

One major problem remained, however. Corruption was not defeated – it has carried on morphing and expanding into new areas since the 1970s.

"The thing about corruption today is that it's far more insidious," said former Met detective Brian Pender. "And I would suggest more dangerous and damaging. The corruption of the 60s and 70s was about policemen just lining their pockets. Today, it's an issue of life and death, because there's more money around drugs, everything like that. So the whole ball game has changed dramatically. It's a tougher world out there.

"The other thing, too, is that in London you have got corruption on the vastest scale."

Line of Duty holds up a mirror to real organised crime

Corruption in *Line of Duty* is on a vast scale as well. Robert Mark may be a role model for Ted Hastings, but Hastings and AC-12 are depicted fighting corruption that is unquestionably contemporary and more alarming than ever.

Central Police in the Midlands city, which is never named, are virtually under siege from the Organised Crime Group. The OCG infiltrates the most senior levels of policing in order to commit crimes, murder opponents and evade justice.

They compromise and blackmail officers of all ranks. They groom people like Matthew Cottan and Ryan Pilkington to become "sleepers" in the police. They use the secrecy of Freemasonry to further their criminal networks of bent officers.

While the propulsive fictional drama is larger than life – with shoot-outs, car chases and attempted murders in the Kingsgate House offices of AC-12 – the corruption is, as we have seen, grounded in reality.

Murder cases and paedophile rings that elude genuine investigation, officers under pressure to meet targets and fill forms, the scapegoating of vulnerable suspects, bent officers assisting criminal ventures – all are taken from the headlines and reimagined in *Line of Duty* storylines.

Central Police is fighting back with resources that have come a long way since A10 brought down the Porn Squad in the 1970s. The drama's AC-12 comes under the Professional Standards umbrella, which includes sister organisations AC-3 and AC-9. They attempt to infiltrate the OCG's online communications and conduct undercover work.

Again, this echoes events in the real world. In the early 1990s, SO11, Scotland Yard's secretive Directorate of Intelligence, was monitoring known crime families and individuals. This came at a time when police operations had been compromised and it was noticed certain criminals appeared to have immunity from police scrutiny and virtual protection from arrest. Some even seemed unfazed by the prospect of arrest, knowing they could buy their way out of prosecution.

All of this suggested that CIB – the Complaints Investigation Bureau, successor to Robert Mark's A10 – was leaking information valuable to criminals and that some staff could not be trusted. A small intelligence cell that became known as the Ghost Squad of around 20 officers was created. In addition to phone taps, surveillance and electronic bugs, a few officers went undercover to spy on suspect colleagues.

In the alternative fiction of *Line of Duty*, Kate Fleming performs the same role for AC-12. She conducts the high-risk role of immersing herself in DCI Tony Gates' team in Series 1 to see what he and his deputies are up to. She attempts to get close to Lindsay Denton in Series 2, while her firearms training comes in useful in Series 3 when she joins Sergeant Danny Waldron's armed squad after they kill a suspect in a suspicious shooting. She plays the mole again in Series 4, shadowing DCI Roz Huntley.

She finally jumps ship after Supt Ted Hastings embarks on his own unauthorised undercover operation and Kate reports him to DCC Andrea Wise. In Series 6, she has joined the Murder Investigation Team at Hillside Lane Station.

By this time, we have ridden the rapids of corruption, double-crossing and betrayals with Kate, Ted and Steve Arnott. In the hands of writer and creator Jed Mercurio, this made for a gripping, action-packed drama. But it is one that also brilliantly captured the ethical and professional challenges facing modern policing. The resignation of Commissioner Cressida Dick in 2022 in the face of multiple Met scandals made clear that overseeing a modern, diverse force up against multiple sophisticated criminal networks is far more daunting than the crime and corruption faced by Robert Mark.

Line of Duty reflects today's more unnerving criminal landscape. The days of bent coppers getting backhanders from criminal mates in smoky pubs are gone. Millions generated by the transnational drug trade and sex trafficking, encrypted communications and remorseless corruption is the world refracted through the plots of the drama.

11 - Beating corruption –
the illusion of success

'God, give me strength'

Line of Duty and the shocking real cases of corruption
Robert Mark did not defeat corruption. He acknowledged it
and confronted it, bringing down high-ranking bent officers in
the process. This was a substantial victory, following Scotland
Yard's long history of downplaying venality and law-breaking in
the force. The problem was that Mark's initial charge against the
many-headed corruption monster fizzled out to some extent.
Even today, making a determined attempt to root out criminal
coppers still sometimes seems to take second place to protecting
the reputation of the police.

Line of Duty encapsulates the problem well when Ted Hastings
moans at the end of Series 4 about the interminable effort needed
to fight corruption, fearing it was becoming a lifetime's work. The
hit BBC drama has become a compelling fictional reflection of
today's brutal criminal networks and the corruption they spread.

Corruption never rests, never goes away. You can nail bent
commanders like Ken Drury and chief superintendents such as
Bill Moody, but the war is not over. If anything, it gets harder
once criminal officers have seen some of their cohort imprisoned
and adapt their corrupt activities to avoid being caught in the
same way.

Former detective Brian Pender told this author that it took a lot of work and skill to build a case against wily bent officers. "Robert Mark addressed the symptoms of the problem," he said. "I'm not quite sure that the Metropolitan Police Service always addressed the root causes."

Scotland Yard started to revert to its complacent default position soon after Mark left the scene. When the beleaguered Operation Countryman corruption probe was wound up in 1982, the Met's Deputy Commissioner, Pat Kavanagh, said the days of the "firm within a firm" were long gone. Corruption was confined to the loner, or rotten apple.

It would appear that complacency had set in further by the 1990s. One detective chief superintendent would say, "Every five or six years [corruption] manifested itself. We put huge resources into it to make sure it was cut out. Then back to normal duty. We felt we'd cured the problem."

Crime was morphing into a bigger, more sophisticated operation during the 1980s. This period saw the emergence of a new breed of gangster, connected through an international underground network of dealers in drugs, human trafficking, fraud, money laundering and more.

At the same time, there seemed to be no proactive effort to confront corruption with the rigour Robert Mark had shown. In their book *Untouchables: Dirty Cops, Bent Justice and Racism in Scotland Yard*, authors Michael Gillard and Laurie Flynn picked out quotes from officers in the newspapers explaining the lack of coordinated action against corruption: "These are our favourites culled from the press clippings: 'We thought it had gone away'; 'We took our eye off the ball'; 'We believed it was almost non-existent'; 'We were not sufficiently alert or skilled to recognise the problem'; 'CIB had become a sleepy hollow'; 'We fell asleep at the wheel'."

A secret 2002 Scotland Yard intelligence report called Operation Tiberius claimed criminals had infiltrated the Met with ease. In 2014, Paul Flynn, Labour MP and member of the Home Affairs Select Committee, was allowed to see the report while the Met supervised the viewing. He said it was "the most deeply shocking document I have read in my life". The MP added, "The report claimed a number of members of the Met Police were involved in criminal conspiracies to commit crime, cover up crime and launder the proceeds." The report revealed that crime syndicates used retired bent cops as go-betweens to buy sensitive intelligence and assistance from serving officers.

Two shocking crimes occurred that caused huge ongoing damage to Scotland Yard's reputation – and both are referenced in *Line of Duty*.

In 1987 private investigator Daniel Morgan was murdered in the car park of the Golden Lion pub in Sydenham, south London. It is suspected he was about to expose corrupt links between local detectives and criminals. The investigation was bungled and the people behind the murder have never been convicted. Despite five inquiries, an inquest and a recent independent panel into the murder and police handling of it, Morgan's family is still campaigning for justice 36 years later.

In 2011 the Met apologised for the police corruption that resulted in the grossly inadequate initial investigation into Morgan's murder, which effectively shielded those responsible. Acting Commissioner Tim Godwin acknowledged that police corruption was a significant cause preventing the killer or killers from being brought to justice. In 2021 Commissioner Cressida Dick apologised again following a damning eight-year investigation by an independent panel into the case. She said it was a "matter of great regret that no one has been brought to justice and that our mistakes have compounded the pain suffered by Daniel's family".

The Morgan case features in a *Line of Duty* scene in episode 2 of Season 6. In it, a colleague of murdered journalist Gail Vella is interviewed by AC-12. The interviewee reveals that Vella, an investigative reporter specialising in corruption cases, had been particularly interested in a podcast about the murdered private detective.

Viewers were quick to pick up on this, several discussing it on social media. One fan Tweeted, "Really interesting how there are elements of real criminal cases in this series of #LineOfDuty – e.g. Jimmy Savile, Jill Dando, Daniel Morgan. It all adds to the realism, and I dare say is writer Jed Mercurio using the show to channel some quite specific social commentary."

No less than seven commissioners have come and gone while the Morgan case has remained unsolved and public dismay continued.

The other case that hit the Met badly was the 1993 murder of teenage student Stephen Lawrence by a racist gang. The 1999 Macpherson Report into the murder and police investigation concluded the Metropolitan Police were guilty of institutional racism. Only two members of the gang, Gary Dobson and David Norris, were finally jailed for the killing in 2012.

As noted in previous chapters, this notorious case is also referenced in *Line of Duty* in the character of Lawrence Christopher, a fictional victim that combines two real-life cases – Stephen Lawrence and Christopher Alder, a former paratrooper who died in police custody.

The Lawrence case blighted the tenure of Sir Paul Condon as Commissioner (1993-2000), as the police struggled to build a case against the teenager's murderers. However, 20 years after Robert Mark's landmark success in convicting the high-ranking detectives running the corrupt Porn Squad, Condon had to acknowledge to a House of Commons select committee in 1997 that corruption was still a serious Met problem: "I honestly believe I command the most honourable large city police service in the world. However, I do have a minority of officers who are corrupt, dishonest, unethical... They commit crimes, they neutralise evidence in important cases, and they betray police operations and techniques to criminals... they are very difficult to target and prosecute."

In 2010 the Serious and Organised Crime Agency (SOCA) started to look into the scale of corruption within the British police. This followed concerns raised by anti-corruption officers that the police were more vulnerable to being targeted by criminals and prone to abusing their powers than their predecessors in the 1970s and 1980s.

Three concerns were considered. One was social-media sites. Officers who identified themselves on these as working for the police could be approached by criminals and fall into inappropriate relationships.

Bodybuilding gyms were another area. Any officers taking steroids in these gyms could come into contact with criminals or drug dealers.

Finally, there was the potential for police officers and civilian staff with access to IT systems and confidential information to cash in by leaking classified data.

In the previous two years before the SOCA assessment, at least 12 officers had been sent to prison for corruption. Others were facing internal investigations or court cases for allegations including spending public money on themselves, having sex with women they had arrested, property scams, stealing, blackmailing people on the police intelligence database, shielding a drugs baron, and passing confidential information to criminals.

Professor Maurice Punch, a criminologist who has written extensively on policing, corruption and accountability, flags up how dodgy dealings have changed since Robert Mark's day. "The old style corruption where groups of detectives had familiar relations with criminals and met in pubs to pass on information has gone because it's too visible, it is too open to scrutiny," he said. "But new opportunities are always being created and exploited."

The level of recent reports and criticism aimed at the Met suggests that while crime and corruption have metastasised, Scotland Yard is still falling short in targeting bent officers, despite the progress in Mark's era.

The stench from the Daniel Morgan controversy continued to waft around. First came the report of the Independent Panel headed by Baroness Nuala O'Loan. Set up by then Home Secretary Theresa May in 2013, it was expected to take a couple of years to look into the murder and botched police investigation. Thanks to hurdles put in its way by the Met – such as dragging out the giving of permission to access police data and documents – the panel ended up taking eight years, finally appearing in 2021. Its report accused the Met of a "form of institutional corruption" and "multiple very significant failings" during the early phases of its murder investigation.

"In failing to acknowledge its many failings over the 34 years since the murder of Daniel Morgan, the Metropolitan Police's first objective was to protect itself," the report stated. "In doing so, it compounded the suffering and trauma of the family."

Once again, the age-old problem of senior figures in Scotland Yard being more concerned about the organisation's reputation than dealing with its corrupt officers was being called out. In addition, it highlighted officers' links to Freemasons – another running theme in *Line of Duty* – as a "source of recurring suspicion".

Theresa May said it was a damning report: "It reveals sadly significant corruption in the Metropolitan Police that took place around the investigation into Daniel Morgan's killer."

Still, the scandal refused to go away. In 2022 a report by Her Majesty's Inspectorate of Constabulary and Fire and Rescue Services (HMICFRS) found the Met's measures to deal with corruption were "dire" and "fundamentally flawed". Many of its criticisms had been raised in the past, but, the report stated, Met promises to fix them had not been kept.

The inspectorate said: "In too many respects, the findings from our inspection paint a depressing picture. The force has sometimes behaved in ways that make it appear arrogant, secretive and lethargic. Its apparent tolerance of the shortcomings we describe in this report suggests a degree of indifference to the risk of corruption."

Bullet points from its bombshell findings were that the Met failed to properly supervise more than 100 recruits with criminal convictions or criminal associates. It found the Met was not certain that staff in sensitive positions, such as child protection and major crime investigations, were vetted properly. More than 2,000 warrant cards in the possession of ex-officers who should not have had them were unaccounted for. Could any of these have been in the hands of criminals, allowing them to pose as police officers?

HMICFRS also found the monitoring of IT systems was poor, meaning corrupt staff could get hold of and sell sensitive information. The report said drugs, cash and exhibits went missing because security arrangements for them were dire.

Matt Parr, who was HM Inspector of Constabulary, said: "Corruption is almost certainly higher than the Met understands."

In view of the recent maelstrom of disasters hitting the Met – Sarah Everard's murder by a Met officer; the insensitive policing of the vigil for her; shocking failings in the investigation of serial killer Stephen Port; the jailing of two officers for photographing the bodies of murder victims Bibaa Henry and Nicole Smallman; racist, sexist and homophobic messages exchanged by officers at Charing Cross nick – it is difficult to argue that the Met has always learned from past mistakes.

Coming five decades after Commissioner Robert Mark threatened to boot out the whole of the CID, it does little for public confidence today that the Met still occasionally appears more concerned with protecting its reputation than acknowledging and aggressively fighting misconduct in its entirety.

All of this provides a compelling backdrop, of course, to the fictional world of *Line of Duty*. According to *Guardian* columnist Simon Jenkins, the message of the drama is serious, that we "risk a collapse in public confidence in the police".

Professor Heather Marquette, who has spent more than 20 years researching corruption, takes a similar line. She says, "Watching *Line of Duty* is practically research... while I appreciate that not everything in the show is as it is in real life, it can help bring corruption research to life."

She says the series shows the process in which decent officers such as Tony Gates can get sucked into breaking the rules, and how "little bites" lead to big corruption. "*Line of Duty* presents a vision of a police service in the UK under significant pressure," she argues. "And it's not just the police. The whole justice system is fraying at the seams in *Line of Duty*. From prison wardens... to the yawning, incompetent duty solicitor who sits idly by while an innocent and vulnerable young man wallows in prison, *Line of Duty* suggests a system that can't effectively fulfil its purpose and risks losing public trust. This is why the work of AC-12 is so important. It's about public trust in the law."

Some political commentators even cite *Line of Duty* as a bellwether of the state of contemporary Britain, with its Party-gate, Wallpaper-gate, lobbying, sexual misconduct, PPE procurement and other scandals. "The British state is like *Line of Duty*, but with no AC-12," said journalist Paul Mason. "While nobody in their right mind thinks *Line of Duty* is real, its metaphoric truth is: when dealing with the commercialised and fragmented British state, you have to assume that everybody is on the make, everyone is gaming the system, everyone has something to hide, and that behind every investigation there is a cover-up."

Jed Mercurio, series creator and writer, has got bolder in depicting a flailing police service as the series has progressed. By Series 6 the spinelessness of politicians in backing anti-corruption probes is examined. Ted Hastings attends a meeting with Police and Crime Commissioner Rohan Sindwhani and Deputy Chief Constable Andrea Wise. Sindwhani and Wise are worried that AC-12 asking questions about DCI Jo Davidson will be seen in the media as another corruption investigation. Sindwhani tells Ted he has discussed the "required optics" of this with Wise, and they want AC-12's activities to be dressed up as a performance review. Hastings is dismayed, but Sindwhani tells him, "Officers of your rank normally appreciate the politics as much as the policing."

To which Hastings gives the reply we probably all hope someone in his position would offer: he is interested in one thing and one thing only – catching bent coppers.

The political message is clear: doing the right thing and exposing police complicity in the murder of Gail Vella takes second place to the force's image and reputation. Ted is being told to help project the right image and don't rock the boat.

In the same episode we see Gail Vella in a broadcast report. She is covering Sindwhani telling the press, "There is no institutionalised corruption in this force." This echoes Commissioner Cressida Dick's denial of institutional corruption following the Daniel Morgan panel's criticisms. Gail Vella then makes a point on air that many critics might have wanted to direct at the real Metropolitan Police hierarchy down the years: "Perhaps Mr Sindwhani has learned that the secret to high office appears to no longer reside in telling the deepest truths, but in telling the most attractive lies."

In the next episode, Ted is told in no uncertain terms to stop "chasing phantoms" and drop his search for "H".

If *Line of Duty* has a defining theme running through it, we probably see it best encapsulated when Ted Hastings learns later in episode 4 of Series 6 that he is for the chop along with AC-12 as we know it. "This is a capitulation to criminality and corruption," he says to his boss, Wise. "What has happened to us? When did we stop caring about honesty and integrity?"

For all its thrills and twists, *Line of Duty* is asking a tough question: can the police be fixed? Former detectives interviewed for this book have their own theories. One was that there should be less political meddling in the police. This was prompted by the perceived lack of support from politicians for the Met Commissioner along with austerity cuts that have seen officer numbers slashed and the selling of training facilities and police stations. Jeff Pope, who was senior producer on the BBC drama *Four Lives*, about Stephen Port, the murderer of four young men, said that when he was researching the project, rather than the suspected rampant homophobia among officers, what he found was that a "shoddy investigation was due to ineptitude, poor systems and underfunding".

One ex-detective suggested today's police needed an FBI-style unit, while another felt something akin to an MI5 team, gathering intelligence on criminal groups and affiliated bent officers was needed. Still another said today's police needed to get back to having good supervision from officers in charge.

The Met's current-day anti-corruption command operates away from the public and media glare for obvious reasons. The HMICFRS report mentioned earlier, while critical of the force, did praise this team, saying it "uses cutting-edge technology, seldom seen elsewhere. We were impressed by the standard of anti-corruption command."

Line of Duty is a celebration of such women and men doing vital work behind the scenes. For all Cressida Dick's dismay at how the series portrayed fictional police, the series depicts Ted Hastings and his AC-12 officers – with all their faults and failings – striving to do the right thing. But the series is also saying that despite their efforts and sacrifices, let's not get misty-eyed about the police. Corruption today is a terrible blight on the service, and corruption has always been eating away at it.

There never was a golden age of virtuous coppering. From the Turf Fraud of 1877 to the Goddard case in 1928, from the postwar Brighton police scandal to the "firm within a firm" of the 1960s and 70s, there have always been groups of bent officers. Sixty-odd years ago, television fictions such as *Dixon of Dock Green* promoted a myth of benevolent policing. Today, *Line of Duty* forensically probes questions closer to what is happening in the real world to a police service struggling with multinational criminal networks and new forms of insidious corruption.

How does police corruption occur? Who gets sucked into becoming a criminal with a warrant card? What does it take to expose devious, ruthless bent officers?

These are the questions that have also fuelled the compelling storylines in the most talked-about British TV drama of recent years.

Series 7 – where could *Line of Duty* go next?

Can the Central Police force in *Line of Duty* be fixed?

Certainly, things had never looked bleaker for the AC-12 team than at the conclusion of Series 6 in May 2021. Ted Hastings appeared to be getting shoved into retirement. Even more dispiriting, most of AC-12's antagonists had finally emasculated the anti-corruption force. With a merger planned between AC-12 and sister units AC-3 and AC-9, and with their budget slashed, the only people left celebrating must be the Organised Crime Group. Most depressing of all, perhaps, highly suspect Philip Osborne was the new Chief Constable, while Hastings' tormentor-in-chief, DCS Patricia Carmichael, was now replacing him.

For more than a year after we learned that Ian Buckells was the fourth man in the "H" quartet, there was no word from *Line of Duty* writer and creator Jed Mercurio on if and when a seventh series would go into production. Reports suggested the leading cast members were keen to open a fresh chapter on *Line of Duty*, even though they have all moved on to major new projects, making finding available time when the stars can come back together for more *Line of Duty* probably trickier than it has been in the past. Adrian Dunbar has his own detective series *Ridley*, Vicky McClure shot the series *Trigger Point* and *Without Sin*, both for ITV, while Martin Compston has been busy with projects including the thrillers *Vigil* and *The Rig*.

Compston best summed up the mood in the immediate aftermath of the near frenzy of fan opinions and theories that engulfed the finale in May 2021. He told *ES Magazine* that the cast needed a break: "The idea that I would never work with all the guys again together would be heartbreaking. But also, with everything that's just gone on this week, I think everybody, including the audience, needs a bit of time away from it. So, we'll see."

It's a given that the BBC would jump at the chance of producing another series of such a ratings jackpot. BBC Chief Content Officer Charlotte Moore commented as Series 6 ended, "Addictive event television, *Line of Duty* has kept the nation guessing for the last seven weeks, so it's no surprise that last night's jaw-dropping finale set a ratings record.

"Jed Mercurio is a master of his craft, and I would like to congratulate him and the entire cast and crew for delivering such an incredible drama series. I'm looking forward to having a conversation with the team about where we go next and what the future of the series might be."

Meanwhile, Mercurio was silent on the subject for much of 2022. He was no doubt fully occupied with new dramas *Trigger Point* (reuniting with McClure) and *DI Ray*. With the writing of each *Line of Duty* series no doubt being a huge undertaking for Mercurio, who has written all 36 intricately plotted episodes, it is understandable that he would want time to clear his creative energies before taking on a new series.

He was non-committal when interviewed by *Radio Times* before Series 6, saying, "We're in a situation where it's not entirely clear that there will be a seventh series. We would hope there could be. But we're having to do our planning coming out of Covid, and a whole bunch of other things, around the idea that these things aren't guaranteed at all now.

"A lot of it depends on the key creatives – that's me and the main actors – finding new stories to tell within that universe."

Finally, just before Christmas of 2022, there was a present for *Line of Duty* followers. *The Sun* quoted a "TV insider" who claimed a three-part special was in the works, with the three main stars, Dunbar, McClure and Compston, all signed up for the return. Filming was likely to go ahead in spring 2023, with a possible broadcast date of Christmas later in the year, or perhaps spring 2024.

There are many avenues down which the new series could venture.

While "H" is now known – Matthew Cottan, Derek Hilton, Gill Biggeloe and Ian Buckells have all been dealt with – a new and obvious question arises. Who was pulling *their* strings? These were all senior figures working on behalf of the Organised Crime Group, but they were not running it. Buckells and DCI Jo Davidson were separately being used by the OCG, with neither apparently knowing the other was a pawn of the same criminals. John Corbett's gang in Series 5 and Jo Davidson in Series 6 communicated with the crime overlord via laptops. So, clearly a major focus of a seventh series could be unmasking the figure who so far has only materialised on a computer screen.

If he had not been strangled to death along with his wife in Spain, former detective chief inspector Marcus Thurwell might be a hot contender as the OCG mastermind. He had had, to put it politely, a rather chequered career in Central Police, his fingerprints appearing on several controversial investigations (or cover-ups).

He was on the investigation into the apparent suicide of Oliver Stephens-Lloyd, the social worker who attempted to expose the abuse scandal at Sands View Boys Home. This was the place where Sgt Danny Waldron had once been a resident. Thurwell's investigation eventually ruled Stephens-Lloyd's death a suicide, but AC-12 would later find signs that he may have been murdered.

Thurwell was later Senior Investigating Officer into the shocking racist murder of Lawrence Christopher. Here it is suspected Thurwell obstructed justice, allowing the young man's attackers to go free. One of them was Tommy Hunter's son, suggesting Thurwell was linked to the OCG chief.

He ended up being pursued for questioning over what went on at Sands View. AC-12 also sought to question him over the Gail Vella murder as Series 6 reached its finale.

However, his badly decomposed body was found and identified by Spanish police. They also found communications equipment at Thurwell's home in the sun that could have been used to forward messages. Was he yet another middleman in the OCG web? Or was he Mr Big, running the show via text and encrypted messages all along? Is he really dead?

As covers go, being dead is a cracker. So, it must be a possibility that Thurwell faked the deaths of himself and his wife. And, let's face it, just having actor James Nesbitt's face on a police photo to depict Thurwell seems a poor use of an actor of his star quality.

Could he turn up alive and kicking in a seventh series, once again a person of interest? Writer Jed Mercurio has said the use of James Nesbitt's image was to "kid" the audience that he might be "H", though that was never their real plan because of his self-imposed rule that "H" had to be someone who had been in *Line of Duty* from Series 1. However, that would not preclude Thurwell being resurrected in future as Hastings and co delve further into the real powers behind the OCG. Thurwell might be a long shot, but *Line of Duty* does love a bit of misdirection.

What of AC-12 itself? It was apparently emasculated in the Series 6 finale by those who had been gunning for it for a long time – new Chief Constable Philip Osborne and DCS Patricia Carmichael, with Supt Ted Hastings pushed out the door into unwanted retirement. That was his reward for a successful investigation. Any viewers who think such vengeful retribution is unrealistic forget that Scotland Yard has down the years appeared to fail to reward successful anti-corruption officers, their exposure of police wrongdoing somehow deemed an unwanted embarrassment.

Could their anti-corruption know-how see Kate Fleming and Steve Arnott pulled back into the new squad? Could Hastings fight to get back? Or might he be involved in a secret intelligence unit, like the real Ghost Squad of the 1990s, set up to spy on suspect officers?

Osborne and Carmichael were more straitjacket than straight-dealing when it came to overseeing AC-12. In Series 1 Osborne attempted to bully Arnott into lying about the police shooting of an unarmed innocent man. As Hastings comments during Series 6 on Osborne becoming chief constable, it is an "outrage" that someone in charge of such a disastrous operation could continue to climb the career ladder right to the top. Osborne was entangled in the Lawrence Christopher case. He was also chummy with Derek Hilton, one of the "H" quartet, working in concert with the OCG.

Carmichael also appears to have been fast-tracked through promotions. Though around a decade younger than Ted Hastings, she is his boss. As Series 6 finished, she has also supplanted him as anti-corruption chief of Central Police. Throughout Series 5 and 6 she was remorseless in attempting to bring down Hastings. But despite her high-flyer status and chilling focus, she is not above making mistakes. It was one of her closest officers, Sgt Tina Tranter, that was revealed in Series 5 to actually be working for the OCG when she tried to assassinate Gill Biggeloe. No doubt had Hastings had Tranter in his closest team, Carmichael would have been unforgiving in suspecting that he too was bent.

So, a big question for a potential new series will likely be where the true loyalties of Osborne and Carmichael are focused. Osborne has multiple question marks over his integrity, but what of Carmichael? Is she just extremely ambitious, or is she, behind the cold smiles, playing another game? Good cop or villain?

The evidence suggests she is not bent but is an enthusiastic please-the-boss type. She is teacher's pet to Osborne, who has shoved Hastings aside and put her in his place.

First, she is eager to show she is protecting the department's budget. When Hastings says Terry Boyle, the intended OCG fall guy in the Gail Vella murder, needs protecting, Carmichael snaps back, "What needs protecting is the anti-corruption budget, which you are going through like there's no tomorrow – which in your case actually does apply." Protecting the budget rather than an innocent man would clearly please her boss, Osborne.

Second, she is keen to play down any idea that there is a network of corrupt officers, always favouring a rogue officer to nail – in the final series, it was Jo Davidson she had in her sights. She decides to drop proceedings against Buckells, who (we soon find out) is actually in cahoots with the OCG. When Hastings talks of a clandestine network of corrupt officers, Carmichael, condescending as ever, adds, "*Hypothetical* network." To slam shut any suggestion of secret gangs, she announces, "We're here to examine DCI Davidson's offending, nobody else's."

This is the classic police hierarchy playbook, blaming the "rotten apple" rather than acknowledging how deep-rooted corruption might be. There was relief in 1969 when just two detectives were convicted for corruption following *The Times'* exposé, when, infamously, one of those under suspicion, DS John Symonds, had revealed there was a "firm within a firm". The firm remained hidden for the time being and Scotland Yard could carry on pretending all was well with the world's finest force.

This is a pattern repeated many times over in the history of UK policing scandals, and Carmichael is a character who exemplifies the type of officer that avoids rocking the boat in order to show their bosses they will protect the force's good name at all costs.

What would be interesting to see is how the relationship between the suspicious Osborne and his eager lieutenant Carmichael might unfold. With Hastings, Fleming and Arnott hopefully still exposing what the OCG do not want exposed, will Osborne be implicated in any kind of relationship with the crime organisation? And how far would Carmichael's loyalty to her patron stretch? It seems at times that she is so desperate to climb the career ladder that she has been willing to turn a blind eye to corruption at senior levels. Or is it that she viewed AC-12 as a threat to her own progress, that any successes for them would reflect badly on her?

Actor Anna Maxwell Martin, showing her versatility in stepping from the comedy of BBC TV's *Motherland*, created one of *Line of Duty*'s most grating villains. Brimming with condescension – "As you were", "Dismissed" – she almost had viewers throwing rotten tomatoes at the screen with her every entrance.

If the series returns, there is huge scope for it to explore what this formidable adversary of Hastings and AC-12 is really up to.

Only Keeley Hawes among the show's major guest stars has appeared across two series as an AC-12 suspect. DI Lindsay Denton returned in Series 3 and foiled "the Caddy" Matthew Cottan in an explosive showdown that was, for many fans, the drama's best season. But could Kelly Macdonald's Jo Davidson be lured out of witness protection, complete with new partner and lovely cottage, to appear in a Series 7 storyline? In a newspaper interview in the summer of 2022, the actor said, "Well, she's not dead, is she? Anything can happen."

And what of bumbling Ian Buckells, who split the *Line of Duty* viewing community when he emerged as a lynchpin in the foursome that constituted "H"? Could he also be wrenched out of protective custody to reveal what more he must know of the OCG?

We need a hero

Line of Duty's universe is rich with potential plot escapades for a new series. Amid the twists and speculation and Ted's outbursts, the drama remains one of television's most powerful thrillers, with a forensic eye on venality and shady dealings in modern Britain.

The theme of this book has been how the much-loved and gripping drama has, from episode 1, also been a veiled exploration of how corruption works and the difficulty of challenging it. This is an aspect of *Line of Duty*'s success that showrunner Jed Mercurio feels strongly about and may be a motivation for him to return to the show.

After Series 6 was broadcast, he acknowledged to the Den of Geek website that the drama had become more reflective of real-world corruption and incompetence. Did he share Ted Hastings' exasperation at the way things were? "When you're doing a drama that's about institutional corruption," Mercurio said, "you have an important decision to make about whether you acknowledge that the environment has changed, or you plough on doing something that's set in an entirely fictional, disconnected world?

"I was thinking about the fact that we aired season one during the summer of the 2012 London Olympics when we were a very small, unheralded police drama buried in the BBC Two schedule. Looking back to that time, it did feel like the country was a very different place. To quote LP Hartley, it's like a foreign country, how it felt then in terms of our national pride and the shared experience of positivity."

One of the changes since then is how corruption has become more visible, he said, citing the rather unclear process around the awarding of PPE contracts during the Covid-19 pandemic to favoured companies that sometimes did not appear to have the expertise to deliver usable products.

The final series stood out as the story most reflective of policing scandals in real life. Notorious investigations referenced were the deaths of Stephen Lawrence, Jill Dando, Daniel Morgan, Christopher Alder and Daphne Caruana Galizia. Mercurio said he would be delighted if viewers looked up these cases as a result of *Line of Duty*. There was even an oblique nod to the killing of teacher Blair Peach during an anti-racism demonstration in Southall, west London, in 1979. In Series 6 we learn that the character Lawrence Christopher was hit and killed with a lead pipe, while illegal weapons including a leaded cosh were found in the lockers of police officers during the Blair Peach inquiries.

"In terms of how we portray police corruption, it's hugely important to us that we find ways of relating it to the real world," Mercurio said. "Otherwise, people will claim that this corruption doesn't exist, so to be able to identify specific real-world correlates is something that's been very important on *Line of Duty* all the way through."

Line of Duty is fictional and may take a few liberties in its depiction of police work, but the deep-rooted corruption that exists in Britain today is not make-believe. It is the infusion of these shocking real events that adds force to the show's thrilling entertainment.

Since Robert Mark was first sounded out about a move from Leicester to Scotland Yard, the efforts of honest detectives and several operations by outside police forces have been thwarted by vested interests in the Met.

Frank Williamson, the Inspector of Constabulary and a dogged, dedicated investigator, was blocked by the Yard's higher-ups from using provincial officers to question Met detectives. He was sabotaged by DCS Bill Moody at every turn during his probe into *The Times*' corruption allegations. He retired, bitter and disillusioned, in 1971. It is easy to envisage Ted Hastings barging out of AC-12's offices in Kingsgate at the end of Series 6 in a similar mood of frustration.

Operation Countryman was another investigation by provincial officers that fizzled out amid allegations of having been nobbled by the Yard and Freemasonry. Initially a probe into alleged collusion between detectives and armed robbers, it ceased in 1982 with Arthur Hambleton, whose Dorset force had run it, saying he was staggered by the corruption they found in London.

In August 2022, the Independent Office for Police Conduct (IOPC) announced that after 35 years, five investigations and an eight-year probe by an independent review, no criminal or disciplinary charges would be brought against officers over the corruption and failures in the Daniel Morgan murder inquiry.

The public get the odd apology, or statements along the lines of "no institutional corruption here", it was just that one rotten apple, the problem has now gone away…

Many people now see through these tired old platitudes. In October 2021, protestors left a barrel of rotten apples outside New Scotland Yard. There was a message with it: "Dear Home Secretary, It's not one bad apple. It's the whole f***ing orchard. Sincerely, women."

On this occasion, the issue being raised by the Women's Equality Party was gender-based violence, prompted by the rape and murder of Sarah Everard by Met officer Wayne Couzens, in addition to 2021 figures showing that 750 police employees had been accused of sexual misconduct over five years. Such protests demonstrate that whether the story is racist behaviour, bribery, homophobia or dodgy investigations, the public no longer believes in the rotten apple excuse.

Long-term conspiracies, detectives working with villains, honest cops foiled – these are the true and disturbing stories, and *Line of Duty* is imbued with them. Spineless politicians (very like *Line of Duty*'s Police Commissioner Sindwhani), careerists (DCS Carmichael), bent cops and lawyers (Cottan, Hilton, Biggeloe, Buckells) can hobble justice and society's protection.

"Public trust can only be maintained when wrongdoing is held to account," Superintendent Ted Hastings tells his bosses.

Jed Mercurio's *Line of Duty* has shown us that justice is slow, that to go down fighting for standards in public office is not a bad way to live, and that vulnerability as you do so is nothing to be ashamed of.

As we sit captivated by the internecine battles facing AC-12, it might be tempting to indulge in a little wish fulfilment. Wouldn't it be nice to have a bloody-minded old scuffler like Ted Hastings running the real Metropolitan Police Service? Someone who does not talk about rotten apples but is, as Robert Mark said so provocatively, intent on ensuring the Met "catches more crooks than it employs".

Hastings for Commissioner – *now* we're sucking diesel.

12 – Casefile

Main and recurring cast

Martin Compston	Detective Inspector Steve Arnott
Vicky McClure	Detective Inspector Kate Fleming
Adrian Dunbar	Superintendent Ted Hastings
Craig Parkinson	Detective Inspector Matthew "Dot" Cottan (Series 1–3)
Neil Morrissey	Detective Constable Nigel Morton (Series 1–3)
Lennie James	Detective Chief Inspector Tony Gates (Series 1)
Keeley Hawes	Detective Inspector Lindsay Denton (Series 2, 3)
Anna Maxwell Martin	Detective Chief Superintendent Patricia Carmichael (Series 5–6)
Daniel Mays	Sergeant Danny Waldron (Series 3)
Thandiwe Newton	Detective Chief Inspector Roz Huntley (Series 4)
Stephen Graham	Detective Sergeant John Corbett (Series 5–6)
Kelly Macdonald	Detective Chief Inspector Joanne Davidson (Series 6)

Supporting

Patrick Baladi	Jimmy Lakewell (Series 4, 6)
Leanne Best	PC Jackie Brickford (Series 3)
Ace Bhatti	Police and Crime Commissioner Rohan Sindwhani (Series 5–6)
Arsher Ali	PC Harinderpal "Hari" Bains (Series 3)
Mark Bonnar	DCC Mike Dryden (Series 2)
Jonas Armstrong	Joe Nash (Series 3)
Taj Atwal	PC Tatleen Sohota (Series 5)
Sherise Blackman	Police Sergeant Ruby Jones (Series 6)
Nigel Boyle	DI/DCI/DSU Ian Buckells (Series 1, 4, 6)
Amy De Bhrún	Steph Corbett (Series 5–6)
Shalom Brune-Franklin	Detective Constable Chloë Bishop (Series 6)
Maria Connolly	Prison Officer Alison Merchant (Series 2, 6)
George Costigan	Patrick Fairbank (Series 3, 6)
Christina Chong	Detective Sergeant/Detective Inspector Nicola Rogerson (Series 2, 3, 6)
Tara Divina	Police Constable Lisa Patel (Series 6)
Rosa Escoda	Amanda Yao (Series 5–6)
Patrick FitzSymons	Mark Moffatt (Series 4–5)
Kwaku Fortune	Detective Sergeant Marks (Series 6)
Aiysha Hart	Detective Sergeant Sam Railston (Series 3–5)
Perry Fitzpatrick	Detective Sergeant Chris Lomax (Series 6)
Paul Higgins	Chief Superintendent/Assistant Chief Constable Derek Hilton (Series 1, 4)

Lee Ingleby	Nick Huntley (Series 4)
Gregory Piper	Ryan Pilkington (Series 1), PC Ryan Pilkington (Series 5–6)
Andrea Irvine	Roisin Hastings (Series 2, 5)
Brian McCardie	Tommy Hunter (Series 1–2)
Gina McKee	Jackie Laverty (Series 1)
Allison McKenzie	DS Jayne Akers (Series 2)
Will Mellor	PC Rod Kennedy (Series 3)
Alastair Natkiel	Lee Banks (Series 5–6)
Tomi May	Miroslav Minkowicz (Series 1, 5)
James Nesbitt	Marcus Thurwell (Series 6)
Andi Osho	Gail Vella (Series 6)
Royce Pierreson	DC Jamie Desford (Series 4)
Tony Pitts	Detective Chief Superintendent Lester Hargreaves (Series 2, 4, 5)
Jessica Raine	DC Georgia Trotman (Series 2)
Rochenda Sandall	Lisa McQueen (Series 5)
Sian Reese-Williams	PS Jane Cafferty (Series 5)
Owen Teale	CI/CC Philip Osborne (Series 1, 6)
Elizabeth Rider	Deputy Chief Constable Andrea Wise (Series 5–6)
Anneika Rose	Police Constable/Police Sergeant Farida Jatri (Series 4, 6)
Polly Walker	Gill Biggeloe (Series 3, 5)
Elliott Rosen	Terry Boyle (Series 1)
Tommy Jessop	Terry Boyle (Series 5–6)
Maya Sondhi	Police Constable Maneet Bindra (Series 3–5)
Jason Watkins	FC Tim Ifield (Series 4)
Maanuv Thiara	Vihaan Malhotra (Series 5)
Susan Vidler	DSU Alison Powell (Series 5)

Line of Duty – case by case

Series 1
Five episodes, first broadcast on BBC Two, June/July 2012

Synopsis
Following a disastrous counter-terrorist raid in which an innocent man is shot dead, Detective Sergeant Steve Arnott refuses to take part in a cover-up of police failings. Because of his stand, he is recruited by Superintendent Ted Hastings to Anti-Corruption Unit 12.

His first case concerns Detective Chief Inspector Tony Gates, who is under investigation for a suspiciously high case clear-up rate. However, this soon expands into an investigation into Gates' relationship with businesswoman Jackie Laverty. Gates covers for her when she is involved in what she says was a hit-and-run accident involving a dog.

Detective Constable Kate Fleming is working undercover in CID, where she observes Gates and his squad, including Detective Constable Nigel Morton and Detective Sergeant Matthew "Dot" Cottan. The AC-12 team soon suspect that Gates is guilty of more than inflating his clear-up stats – that he is also connected to his lover's money-laundering scam. Arnott sees a missing-person report on the disappearance of Laverty's accountant, which Gates subsequently deletes.

Arnott visits a hairdressing premises owned by Laverty and suspects it is part of her money-laundering racket. Gates confronts Laverty over the hit-and-run, in which it was her accountant who was killed, not a dog, as she claimed. Gates realises she is laundering money. He attempts to arrest her, but she persuades him to let her go. While they are together at her house, masked invaders burst in, knock him unconscious, murder Laverty and place Gates' fingerprints on the murder knife. The killers take Laverty's body and the knife away with them.

Hastings and Arnott question Gates, who admits his relationship with Laverty but denies being involved in money laundering. Hastings gets Gates taken off the Laverty case. He is replaced by Detective Inspector Ian Buckells.

Gates is kidnapped by the Organised Crime Group, taken to a warehouse and shown Laverty's body. He is ordered to keep his mouth shut. If not, the knife with his prints will be handed to police. Later, in a call "from Tommy", Gates is told he must help to get Arnott out of the way.

Morton catches Fleming with two mobile phones and realises she is with AC-12. He assaults her.

AC-12 work out the financial link is that Laverty has paid the school fees of Gates' children. Gates is forced to be present when Arnott is lured by the OCG to a derelict building to be tortured by the criminals. Gates is then confronted by a dilemma – to help Arnott or continue serving Tommy Hunter's gang.

Gates rescues Arnott. He insists to Arnott that he never "crossed the line" but was forced to assist the criminals. Gates' career is over, but he is allowed by AC-12 to arrest Tommy Hunter at the Edge Park Golf Club.

Hunter confirms that his gang were responsible for the murder of Laverty as well as three drug dealers earlier in the series. He also says he has someone on the "inside" who always follows orders.

Gates tells Arnott to say he died in the line of duty so his family can get his death-in-service benefits and pension. Arnott is horrified when Gates then jumps in front of a lorry.

Hunter is placed in witness protection.

OCG tentacles
Following Jackie Laverty's murder, Gates is blackmailed by gangster Tommy Hunter, whose modus operandi is to implicate him in Laverty's killing, a ploy the OCG will use throughout *Line of Duty's* remaining series.

Jaw-dropping moment
A desperate Gates sacrifices himself in the final episode for the sake of his family.

Real-world case file
The shooting of Jean Charles de Menezes, 2005, is reflected in the unintended shooting of an innocent man in the opening episode. "Laddering" – Gates is suspected of multiplying spurious charges against offenders that are never tested in court but look good on his clean-up record. Over-stretched young constables Karen Larkin and Simon Bannerjee fail to do their job properly owing to form-filling and police targets. She tries to convince pensioner Alf Butterfield to accept a caution for hitting an underage thug so she won't have to change the paperwork, and she sends the youth, Ryan Pilkington, home even though she knows there is no adult to look after him.

Classic quote
"Best caddy I ever had" – Tommy Hunter, revealing that Cottan is his inside man in the police.

Irritating wee gobshite meter
In Series 3, Ted Hastings says of Steve Arnott to Gill Biggeloe, "He can be an irritating wee gobshite when he wants to be, I'll

give you that." In each series there is a moment when Arnott goes daft or randy...

Such lapses are soon on display in Series 1, when for a time Arnott thinks Gates is a "totally exemplary officer".

Series 2
Six episodes, broadcast on BBC Two, February/March 2014

Synopsis
A secret police convoy carrying a protected witness is attacked on a dark back road by gunmen. The witness is hospitalised and three police officers are murdered. Detective Inspector Lindsay Denton is the sole survivor. How were the criminals able to locate the unscheduled convoy? Was there a police leak? Denton, who organised the convoy without armed support, comes under suspicion from AC-12.

The anti-corruption team discover that Denton had financial troubles because of her mother's illness, making her a potential candidate for corruption to cover her shortage of funds. Fleming declines to be part of the Denton investigation, citing as the reason the time she spent training with one of the dead officers, Detective Sergeant Jayne Akers, omitting the fact that she also had an affair with Akers' husband, Richard. She is replaced by Detective Constable Georgia Trotman. She and DS Steve Arnott grow close and have a sexual relationship. However, Trotman is then murdered at the hospital where the protected witness is being treated. The witness – it is later revealed to be Tommy Hunter – is also assassinated. Denton is ostracised by colleagues and shunted to Missing Persons. Fleming goes undercover to spy on her.

Arnott discovers that the ward nurse, Claire Tindall, was pressured into giving the killer access to Hunter's room.

Meanwhile, Denton investigates the case of missing 15-year-old Carly Kirk. Denton sees through Fleming's cover, assaults her and takes her phone. Denton is later arrested, but she embarrasses AC-12, revealing that Arnott has had a fling with the nurse, exposing Hastings' financial difficulties and alluding to Flemings' affair with Richard Akers. Remanded in custody, Denton is picked on by staff and prisoners.

A story comes out in the media that Deputy Chief Constable Mike Dryden took penalty points for his wife when she committed a driving offence (giving himself an alibi for a sexual encounter).

Denton tells Fleming that she had an affair with Dryden, who is setting her up. DI Cottan learns that DS Akers received a big sum of money before she was killed. AC-12 quiz Dryden, but he brushes them off. Richard Akers tells AC-12 that his wife kept recordings of Tommy Hunter for leverage. These reveal Hunter threatening to expose corrupt officers, including "the Caddy", unless his immunity is maintained.

After Denton's prison transport is ambushed, she falls into the hands of DS Manish Prasad and Trotman's murderer, DC Jeremy Cole, who torture her to find out what she told AC-12. Prasad then kills Cole, whom he calls a "liability", but Denton manages to get away from him. She pins Prasad to a wall using a vehicle and forces him to record a statement implicating Dryden.

AC-12 back Denton's version of events when photos emerge of Dryden and teen Carly Kirk in a sexual encounter. DC Nigel Morton was the officer who flogged the story of Dryden's driving offence to the press. He is subsequently blackmailed by Cottan into claiming the dead officer, Cole, is "the Caddy", a ploy to deflect attention from Cottan.

Arnott finds payoff money hidden among belongings Denton took from her mother. Denton had seen Dryden and Kirk together, as well as Hunter assaulting the young woman. In a flashback, Jayne Akers appeals to Denton to help her get back at Hunter and protect Kirk by facilitating the handing over of the crime boss to his associates, who knew he had threatened to betray them. She agrees and a tracker is placed in Denton's vehicle. Hunter and Akers were killed to protect Cottan's cover, while Denton is left alive to shoulder the blame.

Cottan and Morton call a truce – both agreeing not to rat the other out. Dryden, who was being targeted by the OCG as a future blackmail mark, gets a suspended sentence for perverting the course of justice for lying about his wife's speeding ticket and resigns. Denton is eventually convicted of conspiracy to commit murder and gets a life sentence.

OCG tentacles
Tens of thousands of pounds are finding their way into police pockets to secure access to a witness under police protection. Meanwhile, Deputy Chief Constable Mike Dryden is targeted as part of a potential future blackmail plot.

Irritating wee gobshite meter
Arnott is in serious Jack the Lad mode. He has a relationship with his colleague, Georgia Trotman. After she is murdered, his libido recovers in time for him to have sex with nurse Claire Tindall, a witness in the case – a slip of the trousers that Denton raises to embarrass the AC-12 investigation when she is brought in for questioning. Oh, and then he moves on to an affair with DS Nicola Rogerson.

Jaw-dropping moment
The scene in which Denton turns the tables on AC-12 after she is brought in for questioning, exposing Arnott's affair with

a witness (she has pictures!), Fleming's affair with the husband of dead officer, Jayne Akers, and that Hastings' secret financial problems also make him a prime candidate for blackmail. Red faces all around the table...

Real-world case file
Dryden gets a suspended sentence for perverting the course of justice for a speeding offence said to involve his wife. This recalls the case of former MP Chris Huhne, whose wife took speeding points for him.

Denton accepts money from DS Akers to help entrap Tommy Hunter. There are numerous examples of money exchanging hands for police cooperation in crime, ranging from the Porn Squad "licensing" illegal porn shops in the 1970s, to armed robbers paying detectives to be allowed bail to continue their activities during the same decade.

Classic quote
"I had to do the right thing," Hastings tells his estranged wife, Roisin, meaning he must push on with investigating Dryden, even though Dryden hinted Hastings might get a promotion that would alleviate his financial woes. Ignoring Dryden's hint means Hastings is sacrificing a chance to heal his marriage.

Series 3
Six episodes, broadcast on BBC Two, March/April 2016

Synopsis
Sergeant Danny Waldron and his team of three armed officers come under suspicion after Waldron shoots dead an armed suspect. Waldron claims the man, Ronan Murphy, refused to surrender, but unbeknown to anyone else, Murphy actually

gave up his gun. Waldron orders his colleagues to discharge their guns to make it look as though there was a shoot-out. He intimidates them into backing his version of how Murphy was killed.

Kate Fleming goes undercover to become part of Waldron's squad.

Waldron kills Murphy's uncle, Linus. He then leaves a list of names for Steve Arnott, who has questioned him, to find. Subsequently, during a raid on a drugs house, Waldron is shot to death by squad member PC Hari Bains.

Dot Cottan finds photos of a young Waldron in Waldron's flat, pictured with Ronan and Linus Murphy. Cottan also finds the list of names addressed to Arnott. He destroys it.

One of Waldron's team, PC Rod Kennedy, who had been alarmed at the squad's predicament since the shooting, is found hanged in a warehouse.

Arnott discovers that Waldron had been abused at a boys' home, Sands View, by the Murphys and others. The other firearms team member, PC Jackie Brickford, confesses that Waldron was shot in a struggle.

Cottan frames Bains for Kennedy's murder. In an appeal, Lindsay Denton is found guilty of perverting the course of justice but not conspiracy to murder. She is released. Bains confesses to murdering Waldron on the orders of his OCG handler, whom he has never met.

Former Chief Superintendent Patrick Fairbank claims not to remember any details about investigations into Sands View. He shares a Masonic handshake with Hastings. Cottan attempts to frame Arnott as "the Caddy". Arnott is suspended thanks to Cottan's machinations. Fairbank is identified as one of the abusers.

Denton, suspecting Waldron kept a copy of the list of his abusers, locates it on an internet cafe computer and transfers it to her mobile. Cottan picks her up and drives to an industrial estate and offers her money for the list. She refuses and manages to email the list to Hastings – just before Cottan shoots her dead.

Cottan was using Arnott's car for the murder of Denton, so Arnott is arrested, and evidence implicating him as "the Caddy" is found in his gym bag. Fleming has been working her own undercover operation and discovers Cottan fed a doctored file on Ronan Murphy to AC-12. She also finds CCTV footage of Arnott's car being driven with false plates shortly before Denton's murder.

Fleming then turns up forensic evidence against Cottan – fibres from the rope that killed Kennedy in Cottan's car. Under questioning, the evidence piles up against Cottan, the real Caddy. He sends a text – "Urgent exit required" – and he is sprung from AC-12 in a shoot-out. After a chase involving a getaway car, Fleming shoots one of Cottan's accomplices, but when the wounded man fires at Fleming, Cottan jumps in the way and is himself shot. His dying declaration is recorded, incriminating Fairbank (who is subsequently jailed for 10 years).

Arnott is exonerated, Fleming decorated for bravery and promoted to DS. Morton retires with pension disability benefits, even though everyone knows he is faking his condition.

OCG tentacles
DI Matthew Cottan is the anonymous voice on the phone blackmailing and manipulating Hari Bains on behalf of the OCG.

Irritating wee gobshite meter
Lindsay Denton claims that Steve Arnott had sex with her, a suspect in a corruption/murder investigation. His girlfriend,

DS Sam Railston, is not delighted. Hastings is also infuriated to discover that Arnott mishandled Denton's arrest: "Your team was bossing the game. You went and gave away a penalty."

Jaw-dropping moment
A desperate Cottan shoots Denton when she refuses to hand over the list of abusers at the climax to episode 5.

Real-world case file
The obese councillor who abused boys at Sands View, Dale Roach, is reminiscent of Cyril Smith, former MP for Rochdale. Smith was exposed as a sexual predator of children, many in children's homes and hostels, after his death in 2010. Roach is even seen in a photograph with real-life sexual abuser Jimmy Savile.

The issue of Freemasonry among male officers, and the potential for favouritism and favours between members, has long been contentious because such exchanges would be secret and unaccountable. Hastings and Fairbank share a Masonic handshake, making Fleming and Arnott concerned that their boss might go soft on the abuser. Kate eventually mounts her own undercover op into her AC-12 team, permission for which she went to Supt Madeline Summers at AC-3. This is a precaution by Fleming, because Summers, as a woman, is probably not a Mason and would therefore owe no loyalty to Hastings.

Classic quote
Dot Cottan to Nigel Morton: "People pushed me into the force to do their dirty work from the inside."

Series 4
Six episodes, broadcast on BBC One, March/April 2017

Synopsis

Assistant Chief Constable Derek Hilton pressures Detective Chief Inspector Roz Huntley to charge a man she has caught who is suspected of being a serial killer. Forensic Coordinator Tim Ifield tells her he has doubts about the forensic evidence. He thinks the man is innocent and tells AC-12 there could be a miscarriage of justice. He tells Arnott it looks as though the suspect could be framed. Fleming goes undercover to investigate Huntley.

Huntley turns up at Ifield's flat after work and accuses him of going to AC-12. There is a struggle, she is knocked unconscious but later revives and kills Ifield.

She then continues to pursue a prosecution of the suspect, Michael Farmer. Arnott finds Ifield's body, but Huntley takes control of the murder scene. She sees her own blood there, but later switches her sample for one from Ifield. She also implicates Ifield in the murder of another victim, Leonie Collersdale. Huntley tells Hilton that if Ifield is implicated in murder, the case against her is undermined. She tries to connect Farmer's "crimes" with Ifield.

AC-12 seize evidence by force, as Huntley attempts to concoct evidence linking Ifield and Farmer. Arnott suspects Huntley killed Ifield and questions her husband, Nick. Detective Constable Jamie Desford is assigned to assist Arnott. Arnott later returns to Nick Huntley's office and is attacked by a man in a balaclava. He is thrown down a stairwell.

When questioned by Hastings, Nick realises his car was seen near Ifield's flat the night of his murder. Nick and Roz argue. She appeals to Hilton to call off AC-12. He says he could tell her things about AC-12. They appear to be getting more intimate, but she rejects his advances, suggesting only that they meet again.

A wrist injury Huntley suffered during her fight with Ifield is infected and getting worse. AC-12 find discrepancies in the blood sample she switched. Hastings tells her he will recommend her suspension; she accuses him of sexism. She says she knows Fleming is undercover, and asks Hastings if he is a Mason. He demands to know where she is getting her information. She accuses Fleming of fixing evidence and produces a letter from Hilton recusing AC-12 from the investigation. She meets Hilton at his club, but again rejects him, having apparently got from him the backing she needed to thwart AC-12. PC Maneet Bindra is seen handing Hilton a file later that night in suspicious circumstances.

Body parts of Collersdale are discovered. Bindra leaks to Hilton a recording of Cottan's dying words. Arnott convinces Farmer in prison not to confess to murder, as Huntley suggests he might do. He finds out that Farmer's earlier solicitor was Jimmy Lakewell, who is Nick Huntley's lawyer too.

Roz Huntley's arm begins to smell – at home she collapses. Her husband knows the wound dates from the night of Ifield's murder. He tells Lakewell he believes she killed Ifield. The body parts are shown to have been frozen and buried after Farmer's capture and Ifield's murder. Looking into the forensics again, Arnott finds the Ifield blood sample was contaminated, just like the spatter in the kitchen had been falsified. Huntley is rushed to hospital and her hand is amputated. Arnott suspects Roz is covering up Nick's murder of Ifield. She discharges herself from hospital and arrests Nick for the murder.

Hastings, Fleming and Arnott tell Hilton that evidence was fabricated to implicate Ifield for Collersdale's murder and there is a conspiracy to frame Farmer. Hilton reminds them that AC-12 has been removed from the case, and orders it be handed to an impartial authority. Ordering Arnott and Fleming out, he plays Hastings the tape of Cottan – which Hastings had refused to give him and includes an allusion to "H". Hilton accuses Hastings of being "H" and says he will be served with a Regulation 15 notice.

AC-12 find the blood-stained clothing DCI Huntley had hidden after her fight with Ifield. She is then arrested for Ifield's murder and Lakewell becomes her solicitor.

She admits killing Ifield and framing her husband – but then arrests Lakewell for perverting the course of justice. She has had call data traced from three burner phones. Lakewell used one to tell Hilton of Arnott's visit to Nick – Hilton then used a burner to call Balaclava Man to attack him. Another burner phone was used by the man who planted evidence on Farmer and attacked Arnott. Lakewell was part of a plot to get vulnerable officers to fabricate evidence, so they could subsequently be blackmailed. Roz proves Hilton's involvement by giving the burner phone number he supplied her with – written by him on a napkin – when he tried to get her into bed.

Desford warns Hilton AC-12 are coming for him and he disappears. Arnott and Huntley stop Desford and Lakewell from leaving AC-12's office. Lakewell admits there are several balaclava men – just as a man in a balaclava takes a security guard at gunpoint. Hastings shoots him. Hilton is found dead the next day, an apparent suicide, but the death took place in the same spot as that of Oliver Stephens-Lloyd, the social worker who investigated abuse at Sands View. Hastings frets that untangling the corruption conspiracy is becoming a lifetime's work.

Roz gets 10 years for manslaughter. She and Nick stay married. Lakewell pleads guilty and goes to jail, refusing witness protection.

OCG tentacles

The Assistant Chief Constable, Derek Hilton, is exposed as a high-ranking agent of the Organised Crime Group. He blackmailed PC Maneet Bindra and colluded with DC Jamie Desford. A clue to his motivation comes in Jimmy Lakewell's comment to Arnott: "You think Hilton's top dog. How come he bricks it every time a new body's found?" The implication is that, once again, the OCG has planted an officer's DNA on a murder victim to implicate them – this time it was Hilton. Lawyer Lakewell is also in cahoots with the gangsters.

Irritating wee gobshite meter
Hard not to feel a bit sorry for Steve in this series – he is almost murdered and ends up in a wheelchair.

Jaw-dropping moment
We think Tim Ifield has killed Roz Huntley, as does Ifield himself. He, and we, are in for a shock when he returns to dispose of her – but she revives and kills him.

Real-world case file
DCI Roz Huntley is put under huge pressure and both Lakewell and Hilton know she will jump at a promising suspect – Farmer, who has learning difficulties and is easy to frame. Hastings spots this and says to Hilton: "A detective under that kind of undue pressure can sometimes bend the facts to meet the expectations of his or her superiors." The cause of this kind of blinkered investigation is a form of what is called "confirmation bias". Such cases often feature a high-profile crime, pressure to charge someone, a rush to judgement and ignoring important leads that do not support the guilt of a favoured suspect. Farmer bears a resemblance to the case of Stefan Kiszko, jailed for the rape and murder of 11-year-old Lesley Molseed in 1975. Kiszko, aged 23 but with the mental age of a 12-year-old, confessed after three days of questioning without a solicitor. He spent 16 years

in jail, before new evidence emerged that he was infertile (the attacker's sperm was recovered and tests revealed he could father a child) and witnesses could place him elsewhere on the day of the murder.

Classic quote
Jimmy Lakewell: "There are some people there is no immunity from."

Series 5
Six episodes, broadcast on BBC One, March/May 2019

Synopsis
An armed gang ambushes a police convoy moving drugs. Three officers are killed and a £10 million consignment of seized heroin is stolen. Sergeant Jane Cafferty survives the attack and comes under suspicion. Meanwhile, Hastings, Fleming and Arnott interview Maneet Bindra about her ties with her cousin, OCG snitch Vihaan Malhotra, and leaking AC-12 information to former ACC Derek Hilton, who passed it to the OCG. Hastings says she will be given a Red Notice, her police career over. Bindra contacts the OCG and offers assistance in exchange for her cousin to be spared a violent time in prison. John Corbett, working undercover inside the OCG but now apparently gone rogue, finds that the burner phone she is using has been bugged – Bindra actually wanted to redeem herself by collecting evidence against the OCG to betray the criminals to the police. She is murdered on the same quayside as Oliver Stephens-Lloyd and Derek Hilton.

Lisa McQueen, John Corbett's OCG deputy, pretends to be a nurse so she can see recuperating Cafferty and assure her she is safe from the OCG. Cafferty gives McQueen new inside information for Corbett regarding a police convoy of seized weapons. Lee Banks later visits her and gives her a big sum of money. However, AC-12 is watching and arrest Banks. The bribe is found, and Cafferty is also arrested. She confesses to Arnott and Fleming that she had passed details of police operations to the OCG, having been blackmailed by the gang over an extramarital affair she had been in.

Elsewhere, Corbett convinces Arnott he has not gone rogue. We also learn that before joining the police, Corbett had worked in printing. He uses that expertise to help the OCG's forging operations.

Investment manager and former detective Mark Moffatt meets Hastings to discuss his disastrous real estate deal and gives him a large brown envelope. Hastings' wife, Roisin, insists they push on with divorce.

Arnott reveals to Hastings and Fleming that he has met Corbett. They are shocked but agree to let him carry on dealing with Corbett. AC-12 raid a block of flats used for sex trafficking and prostitution. Corbett informs Arnott of a planned raid by his gang on the Eastfield Police Storage Facility. He claims a bent senior policeman will be there. A shifty-looking Hastings is seen disposing of a laptop. During the Eastfield raid, Corbett shoots the OCG's stooge officer – DCS Lester Hargreaves – claiming later he only wanted to frighten him. However, his twisted logic is that it is only bent cops who are being killed. Later, Corbett tortures Roisin Hastings at her home (apparently to get her to reveal that Ted has money troubles).

During dinner, flirtatious legal counsel Gill Biggeloe invites Hastings to retire. Later, he feels guilty about Roisin's attack, telling Biggeloe, "My wife was attacked at exactly the same time I was with you. If that's not a sign, I don't know what is."

AC-12 learns that Corbett's early upbringing was in Northern Ireland.

Arnott meets Corbett in a public place, backed up by a hidden armed team. Corbett tells Arnott he attacked Roisin (he thinks Ted is "H"). Hastings orders Arnott to shoot Corbett – Arnott defies Ted. AC-12 uses the identity of "H" to contact the OCG via a laptop. The gang is moving a group of trafficked women. Corbett plans to free them with Lisa McQueen's help and get out of the OCG. However, Corbett is betrayed, isolated and murdered.

The bodies of Corbett and Jackie Laverty, the corrupt businesswoman murdered in Series 1, are found dumped together. Operation Pear Tree into links between criminals and police is taken away from AC-12 – "You've had your time, Ted," says Deputy Chief Constable Andrea Wise. Hastings goes rogue and infiltrates the OCG, convincing McQueen and Miroslav Minkowicz he can find buyers for goods from the Eastfield raid. Armed officers appear, McQueen is arrested, Minkowicz shot dead. AC-12 learn Hastings made a surreptitious visit to Lee Banks in prison. Enter Detective Chief Superintendent Patricia Carmichael, who suspends Hastings and charges him with conspiracy to murder Corbett.

Carmichael grills Hastings in the bubble about £50,000 found in his hotel. "I'm being framed," he pleads. Fleming and Arnott make a breakthrough when they discover that Gill Biggeloe was involved in Corbett being chosen for undercover work on Operation Pear Tree – she also pitched Hastings to him as someone to target because of his association with Corbett's mother back in Northern Ireland. She was suspected by IRA paramilitaries of being an informer and murdered. Biggeloe used this to imply to Corbett that Hastings was responsible for his mother's disappearance. It turns out Biggeloe became involved with the OCG during her time as a defence solicitor. She appeals to the OCG to extract her from AC-12, but this fails. Instead,

PS Tina Tranter tries to stab her in the ladies' toilet but is shot by Arnott.

The epilogue reveals that Ryan Pilkington (the juvenile thug in Series 1) is becoming a rookie police officer, Biggeloe is receiving immunity and a new identity, while Hastings is given a final warning over his dubious unofficial approaches to the OCG. Mark Moffatt claims he gave Hastings £100,000, double what was found in Ted's hotel room, raising the question of what happened to the other £50,000. Hastings is seen approaching Corbett's widow at the end with an envelope, perhaps out of a mixture of guilt at having inadvertently exposed John Corbett to the OCG during his visit to Lee Banks, and because he could not do more to help Corbett's mother as a young officer in Belfast.

OCG tentacles

Biggeloe, Tranter and Moffatt are all OCG pawns. Moffatt, the former copper now working for the Kettle Bell firm – and probably recruited to the OCG by Gill Biggeloe – is a lead player in the attempt to frame Ted Hastings by giving him the unsolicited £100,000, which of course looks suspiciously like a bribe. When she tries to stab Biggeloe in the ladies', PS Tina Tranter reveals herself to be an OCG plant, though it is never explained how she was enticed into its ranks. This series' big reveal is that Gill Biggeloe – who has in past episodes variously attempted to seduce, divert and undermine Ted – has been doing the OCG's bidding all along, having been lured into their orbit back when she was a defence lawyer, representing members of the crime group.

Irritating wee gobshite meter

For at least the second time during whole run of *Line of Duty*, Ted Hastings brands Steve Arnott a "wee gobshite" when he ignores the superintendent's order to shoot John Corbett and the undercover man gets away (the first time is in Series 3).

Jaw-dropping moment
The scene when John Corbett tries to break free of the OCG with Lisa McQueen in episode 4. He pulls a gun, also intending to set the enslaved sex workers free, but is ambushed and has his throat cut by Ryan Pilkington.

Real-world case file
Lisa McQueen pays off guards and drivers at the Eastfield police depot, clearing the way for the gang to raid the premises and steal £50 million worth of contraband drugs, illicit cash and other goods. This brings to mind the cosy relationship between a coterie of City of London detectives and armed robbers during the 1970s. This resulted in criminals paying detectives not to object to bail and for evidence to be watered down. Armed police units were also distracted so that a robbery could go ahead without fear of a confrontation with armed officers.

Gill Biggeloe undermining Ted Hastings and AC-12 to help the OCG highlights the real-world problem of bent lawyers. This was attacked by Robert Mark. He controversially criticised lawyers who were paid lavishly by criminals to invent spurious defences and alibis, and to suborn witnesses to commit perjury.

Classic quote
On being told of Corbett's plan to raid the heavily guarded Eastfield police depot, an incredulous Ted Hastings says: "What's he got backing him up there, a panzer division?"

Series 6
Seven episodes, broadcast on BBC One, March/May 2021

Synopsis

Detective Chief Inspector Jo Davidson is in charge of the Murder Investigation Team's (MIT) Operation Lighthouse, the inquiry into the murder of journalist Gail Vella. She is told that a Covert Human Intelligence Source (CHIS) has identified a suspect, a man identified as "Ross Turner". A raid to arrest him at his flat is delayed by Detective Superintendent Ian Buckells, who wants "executive-level sign-off". It is further held up the next day when an armed team, along with Kate Fleming (now with MIT), are sidetracked by Davidson to tackle a robbery at a bookie's shop. Finally, the raid on the suspect's flat in Beechwood House goes ahead and the police find a man there who is vulnerable and has Down's syndrome. He identifies himself as Ross Turner, but under questioning it turns out he is Terry Boyle. He also does not live at the flat but elsewhere in the Kingsgate area. This flat has been deep-cleaned, but photos and articles about Gail Vella are found, suggesting Boyle may have been stalking her. Gunshot residue is found in his clothes.

Sergeant Farida Jatri reports Davidson's suspicious delay and conduct to Steve Arnott. Later, Davidson arrives at Jatri's flat – the pair have just had a painful breakup. The body of the CHIS informant is found. Hastings gives Arnott the go-ahead to investigate Davidson. Arnott tells Fleming she needs to help AC-12 with this, but she is reluctant.

Arnott and his new partner, Detective Constable Chloë Bishop, discover Vella was working on a podcast about police corruption. Known criminal Carl Banks, whose fingerprints were found in the Beechwood House flat where Boyle was supposed to be living, is discovered stabbed to death, with the murder weapon nearby, revealing the CHIS's prints, and an OCG killing is suspected.

AC–12 try to seize Operation Lighthouse files, but Davidson thwarts this, delaying their inquiry. Hastings and Arnott think their former colleague Fleming tipped her off. At the home of Steph Corbett, widow of John Corbett, Steph sees that Arnott is addicted to painkillers – a result of the attack he suffered in Series 4.

Davidson is arrested and tells AC–12 that everyone who had access to the CHIS information should be looked into. Jatri is arrested when a search of her house turns up a stash of burner phones. She says she is being framed. Davidson is released. She receives a burner phone. In her car she breaks down in tears.

Boyle is brought in for further questioning, but Davidson stops the interview when it seems he is about to reveal something about the man who committed the murder. After, Pilkington and PC Lisa Patel drive him home. Pilkington changes the route and forces the car into a reservoir. He drowns Patel before trying to kill Boyle. However, Fleming was following them and arrives before that can happen. She reports to AC–12 that Pilkington's window was open, suggesting he may have planned to escape the sinking car (the doors would not open underwater if it was shut).

Arnott recognises Pilkington, and Fleming then recalls interviewing him when he was a juvenile accomplice of the OCG. Arnott tries to break his painkiller habit. He spends the night at Steph's house, and when he is alone he locates a large amount of money hidden there. Boyle's missing freezer is found on a dump – it has samples of Jackie Laverty's blood in it.

It emerges that Buckells had a sexual relationship with Deborah Devereux, the witness who implicated Boyle. AC–12 investigates him. In her well-locked-up flat, Davidson sends a message on her laptop to someone, saying that everything has been dealt with.

AC-12 charges Buckells. DCC Andrea Wise tells Hastings AC-12 is being merged with AC-3 and AC-9, its budget will be slashed by 90 per cent, and he should consider retiring to dodge further potential disciplinary charges.

Davidson sends a message to her mystery contact: "I'm finished." Arnott realises one of the voices on a recording from Gail Vella's office is that of Jimmy Lakewell, the lawyer in jail because of his OCG ties. Arnott and Bishop interview him there, but he refuses to talk. They then shift him to protected custody but during the drive there his convoy is ambushed by the OCG. Pilkington resists Davidson's attempt to remove him from Operation Lighthouse. Lakewell, who survived the ambush, is subsequently murdered back in prison, while Buckells is forced to watch.

Bishop looks into connections between Lawrence Christopher – victim of a racist killing in Central Police custody – and Gail Vella.

Fleming is told by AC-12 that DNA evidence shows Davidson is related to Tommy Hunter, perhaps as a result of incest. Arnott learns that the £50,000 in Steph Corbett's possession was given to her by Hastings, and he tells Fleming about this. Pilkington is spotted making a call to the OCG using a concealed mobile. Bishop briefs Hastings and Arnott about Lawrence Christopher, and Arnott learns that DCI Marcus Thurwell was implicated in a case involving abuse at Sands View Boys Home that was suppressed. This is the quagmire about which Vella was asking questions.

Davidson is ordered to "get rid" of Fleming, but Fleming resists being transferred. Bishop discovers that Vella tried to speak to several former AC-12 suspects – Roz Huntley, Manish Prasad, Hari Bains. Only Lee Banks agreed to speak to her. Arnott interviews him and is stunned to be told Hastings tipped off the OCG about a mole in their ranks. Davidson lures Fleming to an isolated spot, but Fleming has alerted Arnott to this rendezvous. Fleming and Pilkington face each other with guns, and Fleming kills him.

DCS Patricia Carmichael assumes command of AC-12, revealing to Hastings that the unit's vehicles have been fitted with tracking devices because neither she nor Chief Constable Philip Osborne trust Hastings' team. Interviewed by Carmichael, Davidson is disturbed on hearing of her incestuous parentage but initially refuses to answer questions. She does, however, claim it was she who shot Pilkington, not Fleming. She finally acknowledges she has been coerced by the OCG. Carmichael does not seem interested in this aspect of her testimony. Davidson is charged and placed in custody, while Fleming is cleared.

Police in Spain search a property suspected to be Marcus Thurwell's – two decomposed bodies are found. Two guards appear in Davidson's prison cell, notice CCTV cameras and leave. It would appear she is in danger from guards under orders from the OCG.

The murder team have been searching for a workshop where firearms may have been made and used in the Vella murder. The first one they checked was empty, but Fleming now orders the floor of it to be excavated. Weapons used to kill Vella, Jackie Laverty and Maneet Bindra are found. AC-12 intercept a message that Davidson, who is about to be transported from prison to AC-12 for further questioning, should be eliminated. The hitmen and guards who were to carry out the killing are caught.

Davidson is offered witness protection. She reveals she had thought convicted paedophile and former chief superintendent Patrick Fairbank was her father.

During questioning, Buckells outs himself as the Fourth Man in the "H" quartet. He requests immunity and witness protection. Instead, he is arrested. Hastings admits giving the bribe money to

Steph Corbett. He acknowledges he may have unintentionally exposed undercover officer John Corbett to the OCG. Davidson begins a new life with her girlfriend.

Osborne hushes up all the corruption surrounding Buckells by getting public interest immunity for proceedings against the disgraced detective, so that evidence of police criminality can be kept out of court. Osborne begins dismantling AC-12 and slashing the budget for the new anti-corruption unit.

OCG tentacles
The criminal group has had two high-level "sleepers" working for it in Central Police – DCI Jo Davidson and her boss, DSU Ian Buckells, the Fourth Man. The OCG also has its lackeys in the prison service, hence the murder of Jimmy Lakewell, the attack on PS Farida Jatri, and the planned assassination of Davidson. The shadowy network not only got Davidson to sabotage the investigation into the murder of Gail Vella, they also murdered the journalist to prevent her exposing the truth about the killing of Lawrence Christopher (one of whose killers was the son of former OCG boss Tommy Hunter).

Irritating wee gobshite meter
Steve Arnott felt that Ian Buckells "couldn't organise a piss-up in a brewery". It fell to Kate Fleming to spot the rat: "Yeah, but that's his cover." Buckells turned out, of course, to be the Fourth Man in the "H" quartet.

Jaw-dropping moment
The night-time Mexican stand-off between Kate Fleming and Ryan Pilkington. Shots are fired… but the audience is left hanging on for the next episode to see who is still standing. It is, of course, Kate.

Real-world case file

Jo Davidson is under suspicion for her handling of Operation Lighthouse, the investigation into the murder of journalist Gail Vella. Showrunner Jed Mercurio said he was thinking of assassinated Maltese journalist Daphne Caruana Galizia, who wrote about high-level corruption, when he created the Vella character. Caruana Galizia's maiden name was Vella. She died in 2017 when a bomb in her car exploded.

The unsolved murder of private investigator Daniel Morgan in 1987 is mentioned in episode 2.

Another suspicious investigation in Series 6 is the one into the historical murder of Lawrence Christopher – a composite of the names of real-life victims Stephen Lawrence and Christopher Alder. Lawrence, aged 18, was murdered by a racist gang in 1993. Former paratrooper Alder was "unlawfully killed" in police custody in 1998 while handcuffed and lying on the floor. A tape later emerged of police making monkey noises as he lay dying. In the series, DC Chloë Bishop reports, "Custody suite video shows the officers mocking Christopher while he lay unresponsive in his cell." The police investigations into the deaths of these two innocent men were heavily criticised, suggesting they inspired the suspiciously lacklustre investigations in similar circumstances in *Line of Duty*.

A line spoken by Ted Hastings sparked a little controversy during this series: "More likely to be the gunman than the local oddball." This was a reference to Terry Boyle, the man with Down's syndrome who is being set up to take the blame for the murder of Gail Vella. There was criticism in the media that Hastings described Boyle as an "oddball", to which writer Jed Mercurio said the term was a reference to cases in which police had picked on a local loner or eccentric and made them a suspect. Barry George, the man wrongly imprisoned for the

1999 murder of TV presenter Jill Dando, agreed that that was how police had viewed him. His sister, Michelle Diskin Bates, told the *Daily Mirror* that he agreed with the show's creator, and she added that Mercurio should be "lauded not reviled" for highlighting such miscarriages. Mercurio said the term was meant as a reference to the Dando case, not learning difficulties.

Classic quotes

Ted Hastings on being told AC-12 was having its resources cut by 90 per cent: "This is a capitulation to criminality and corruption... What has happened to us? When did we stop caring about honesty and integrity?"

Ian Buckells on being arrested: "This is bollocks. Total bastard bollocks."

Abbreviations

Line of Duty's plots are full of red herrings, misdirection, double-dealing and some very dishonest people. To stay on top of the action, it helps to learn the lingo used in this world.

Police Units
AC-12: Anti-Corruption Unit 12
AC-3: Anti-Corruption Unit 3
AC-9: Anti-Corruption Unit 9
CID: Criminal Investigation Department
MIT: Murder Investigation Team

Ranks and job titles
PCC: Police and Crime Commissioner
CC: Chief Constable
DCC: Deputy Chief Constable
ACC: Assistant Chief Constable
DCS: Detective Chief Superintendent
CS: Chief Superintendent
DSU: Detective Superintendent
Supt: Superintendent
DCI: Detective Chief Inspector
CI: Chief Inspector
DI: Detective Inspector

PS: Police Sergeant
DS: Detective Sergeant
DC: Detective Constable
Sgt: Sergeant
PC: Police Constable
UCO: Undercover Officer
SIO: Senior Investigating Officer
SOCO: Scene of Crime Officer
FI: Forensic Investigator
FC: Forensic Coordinator

Operational
OCG: Organised Crime Group
ANPR: Automatic Number Plate Recognition
CHIS: Covert Human Intelligence Source
PACE: Police and Criminal Evidence Act (1984)
PNC: Police National Computer

Organisations
IPCC: Independent Police Complaints Commission
IOPC: Independent Office for Police Conduct
CPS: Crown Prosecution Service

Sources

David Ascoli, *The Queen's Peace*, Hamish Hamilton, 1979

Barry Cox, John Shirley, Martin Short, *The Fall of Scotland Yard*, Penguin Books, 1977

Martin Fido, Keith Skinner, *The Official Encyclopedia of Scotland Yard*, Virgin Books, 1999

Michael Gillard, Laurie Flynn, *Untouchables: Dirty Cops, Bent Justice and Racism in Scotland Yard*, Bloomsbury Publishing. Kindle Edition, 2012

Dick Hobbs, *Doing the Business: Entrepreneurship, the Working Class, and Detectives in the East End of London*, Clarendon Press, 1988

Deborah Jermyn, *Prime Suspect*, BFI/Palgrave Macmillan, 2010

Gilbert Kelland, *Crime in London: From Postwar Soho to Present-Day Supergrasses*, Grafton Books, 1987

Dick Kirby, *The Brighton Police Scandal: A Story of Corruption, Intimidation and Violence*, Pen & Sword Books, 2021

Graeme McLagan, *Bent Coppers: The Inside Story of Scotland Yard's Battle Against Police Corruption*, Orion Books, 2004

Jackie Malton (with Hélène Mulholland), *The Real Prime Suspect: From the Beat to the Screen. My Life as a Female Detective*, Endeavour, 2022

Sir Robert Mark, *In the Office of Constable, an Autobiography*, Collins, 1978

James Morton, *Bent Coppers: A Survey of Police Corruption*, Warner Books, 1998

Maurice Punch, *Police Corruption: Deviance, Accountability and Reform in Policing*, Routledge, 2011

Maurice Punch, Stan Gilmour, *Police Corruption: Apples, Barrels and Orchards*, Centre for Crime and Justice Studies, 2010

Robert Reiner, *The Politics of the Police*, Oxford University Press, 2010

Neil Root, *Crossing the Line of Duty: How Corruption, Greed and Sleaze Brought Down the Flying Squad*, The History Press, 2019

Graham Satchwell, Winston Trew, *Rot at the Core: The Serious Crimes of a Detective Sergeant*, The History Press, 2021

Lawrence W Sherman, *Police Corruption: A Sociological Perspective*, Anchor Books, 1974

Barbara Weinberger, *The Best Police in the World: An Oral History of English Policing from the 1930s to the 1960s*, Scholar Press, 1995

David I Woodland, *Crime and Corruption at the Yard: Downfall of Scotland Yard*, Pen & Sword Books, 2015

Television
Bent Coppers: Crossing the Line of Duty, BBC Two, 2021

Online resources
Three websites provide fantastic in-depth scrutiny of *Line of Duty* and its dense plots:

denofgeek.com
lineofduty.fandom.com
radiotimes.com

Acknowledgements

Special thanks to those who generously gave their time, and in some cases their hospitality, to speak to me: Jackie Malton, Don Williams, George Thomson-Smith, Dick Kirby, Brian Pender, Michael Taylor. All had fascinating careers and offered invaluable insights and trenchant opinions on policing since the 1970s.

The team at Mardle Books has been superb to work with: Jon Rippon, Duncan Proudfoot, Fritha Saunders, Mel Sambells. Special thanks to Jo Sollis, the guiding hand and support behind each book I've worked on.